Contents

Maynooth Research Guides for Irish Local History: Number 2

Church of Ireland records

Raymond Refaussé

FOUR COURTS PRESS

Set in 10.5 pt on 12.5 pt Bembo for
FOUR COURTS PRESS LTD
7 Malpas Street, Dublin 8, Ireland
e-mail: info@four-courts-press.ie
http://www.four-courts-press.ie
and in North America by
FOUR COURTS PRESS
c/o ISBS, 920 N.E. 58th Avenue, Suite 300, Portland, OR 97213.

A catalogue record for this title
is available from the British Library.

ISBN (10 digit) 1–85182–963–6
ISBN (13 digit) 978–1–85182–963–7

Printed in England
by Antony Rowe Ltd, Chippenham, Wilts.

Church of Ireland records

Maynooth Research Guides for Irish Local History

GENERAL EDITOR Mary Ann Lyons

This book is one of the Maynooth Research Guides for Irish Local History series. Written by specialists in the relevant fields, these volumes are designed to provide historians, and specifically those interested in local history, with practical advice regarding the consultation of specific collections of historical material, thereby enabling them to conduct independent research in a competent and thorough manner. In each volume, a brief history of the relevant institutions is provided and the principal primary sources are identified and critically evaluated, with specific reference to their usefulness to the local historian. Readers receive step by step guidance as to how to conduct their research and are alerted to some of the problems which they might encounter in working with particular collections. Possible avenues for research are suggested and relevant secondary works are also recommended.

The General Editor acknowledges the assistance of both Dr Raymond Gillespie, NUI Maynooth and Dr James Kelly, St Patrick's College, Drumcondra, in the preparation of this book for publication.

IN THIS SERIES

Terence A.M. Dooley, *Sources for the history of landed estates in Ireland* (2nd ed., forthcoming)

Raymond Refaussé, *Church of Ireland records* (2nd ed., 2006)

Patrick J. Corish and David C. Sheehy, *Records of the Irish Catholic Church* (2001)

Philomena Connolly, *Medieval record sources* (2002)

Brian Gurrin, *Pre-census sources for Irish demography* (2002)

E. Margaret Crawford, *Counting the people: a survey of the Irish censuses, 1813–1911* (2003)

Brian Hanley, *A guide to Irish military heritage* (2004)

Jacinta Prunty, *Maps and map-making in local history* (2004)

Brian Griffin, *Sources for the study of crime in Ireland, 1801–1921* (2005)

Toby Barnard, *A guide to sources for the history of material culture in Ireland, 1500–2000* (2005)

Illustrations

Acknowledgments

This guide has been written from the background of almost twenty-five years as the archivist of the Church of Ireland and I am enormously grateful to many clergy and laity, members of staff in Church of Ireland House, Dublin, and colleagues and researchers in the Representative Church Body Library from whom I have learned much of what follows. I am indebted to my colleagues Susan Hood, Mary Furlong and Pam Stanley for much practical advice and assistance, to Colum O'Riordan for information on the Irish Architectural Archive, and to the Director of the National Archives for permission to reproduce illustration four.

I am grateful to Raymond Gillespie who first suggested this project to me and especially to the series editor, Mary Ann Lyons, and Alison O'Keeffe, who read the complete text, made valuable suggestions and saved me from errors.

I am especially grateful to Four Courts Press for agreeing to publish a second edition of the guide which has allowed me to correct errors, smooth out infelicities, add fresh information in response to suggestions from those who used the first edition, and bring the citations of published works up to date.

My principal debt, however, remains to the members of the classes of the MA in Local History course in NUI Maynooth who have, in turn, been bored by topics which I thought to be fascinating, enthralled by things which I believed to be of no account, and who have continued to ask me questions to which I did not know the answers. To them this guide is cheerfully dedicated.

1 The provinces and dioceses of the Church of Ireland

Introduction

The Church is the only institution in Ireland that has survived from the earliest times to the present day, predating central government, municipal corporations and the handful of educational and fraternal bodies that have been extant since the Middle Ages. Its longevity combined with its sustained presence in almost every corner of the country suggests that it is, or has been, the most profound influence in the formation of Irish society. Since the sixteenth century the Church in Ireland has been divided, and of those parts of the Church which withdrew their allegiance from Rome, the most historically significant is the Church of Ireland.

The Church of Ireland is an anglican or episcopalian church. It is a reformed catholic Church: reformed, in that it is opposed to any teaching and practice that appears to be contrary to scripture and to the teaching of the primitive Church; and catholic, in that it is in possession of a continuous tradition of faith and practice based on the scriptures and early tradition, and enshrined in the catholic creeds, the sacraments and the three-fold ministry of deacons, priests and bishops. It is, legally at least, the lineal descendant of the Celtic Church, for following the Reformation it was established as the official Church of the State, a situation which continued until the late nineteenth century when disestablishment reduced its status to that of a voluntary Christian community. These three phases of development – the pre-Reformation Church, the established Church, and the disestablished Church – provide convenient divisions under which to examine the administration of the Church of Ireland and the records which that administration produced.

However, the archives (the papers which have been accumulated in the process of the official administration of the Church), the manuscripts (the records of individuals and organizations which, although Church of Ireland in orientation, are not part of the Church's official archives but complementary to them) and the non-written primary sources (gravestone and memorial inscriptions, church plate, portraits and stained glass) of the Church of Ireland are not all held in one repository. Neither are they all under the control of the Church. Consequently it is not possible to describe and analyze Church of Ireland records as one distinct collection. What follows, therefore, is an overview of the Church's administration and the archives and manuscripts that it produced; a guide to the various published catalogues and printed editions; and an introduction to the principal repositories in which Church of Ireland records are to be found with an indication of the types of material contained in these institutions.

ABBREVIATIONS

NLI	National Library of Ireland
RCBL	Representative Church Body Library
RIA	Royal Irish Academy
PRONI	Public Record Office of Northern Ireland
TCD	Trinity College Dublin

CHAPTER I

The administration, archives and manuscripts of the Church of Ireland

THE CHURCH IN IRELAND: FROM EARLIEST TIMES TO THE REFORMATION

The elements of what most people would consider to be the essentials of church administration – bishops, dioceses and parishes – are the product of the early Christian Church.[1] The term 'bishop' is an Anglo-Saxon corruption of the Greek word *episcopus* which means overseer. In the early Church the terms 'bishop' and 'priest' seem to have been interchangeable, but by the beginning of the second century the threefold ministry of bishops, priests and deacons was becoming defined, and by the middle of the century all the leading centres of Christianity would appear to have had bishops, the particular functions of whom were to ordain to holy orders and to confirm the baptized. The unit of administration which a bishop governed was the diocese, and in the early Church, when Christianity was an urban religion, dioceses were small in extent, covering only the principal towns and cities. However, as the Church expanded into rural areas the limits of the dioceses were extended until all the civilized world was, notionally at least, within the jurisdiction of a diocesan bishop. In the western Church the term *parochia,* which is, of course, the origin of the word 'parish', was used in some places to describe the bishop's area of jurisdiction, but from the later fourth century it came to be applied to the subdivisions of the diocese which the bishop put in the charge of resident priests. By the seventh century the parochial system had spread as far as England.[2] In Ireland, however, ecclesiastical jurisdictions were arranged differently. The Celtic Church seems to have been more monastic than diocesan, and monasteries rather than parish churches were the centres of Christian life. Bishops, being needed to ordain and confirm, were a part of the Irish ecclesiastical polity but generally lived in the monasteries.

The written legacy of the Celtic Church lies not so much in what we would understand as archives but in monastic annals such as the Annals of Inisfallen and the Annals of Tigernach, both with origins in the eleventh century, which can provide valuable data on chronology, and hagiographical lives of the saints like St Fin

---

1 For explanations of ecclesiastical terminology, with bibliographical references, see F.L. Cross & E.A. Livingstone (eds), *The Oxford dictionary of the Christian church* (3rd ed., revised, Oxford, 2005). 2 For a short introduction to the parish system see G.W.O. Addleshaw, *The beginnings of the parochial system & the development of the parochial system from Charlemagne (768–814) to Urban II (1088–1099)* (London, 1954). For a fuller treatment see N.J.G. Pounds, *A history of the English parish* (Cambridge, 2000).

Barre of Cork and the various St Patricks, which can often give an interesting sense of a locality. Also valuable are liturgical manuscripts ranging from the Cathach, an austere sixth-century psalter, to the splendidly illuminated ninth-century gospel book, the Book of Kells. The provenance of such volumes has often much to say about the localities and societies in which they were created while their subsequent ownership frequently testifies to the value attributed to them by later generations. Insofar as these manuscripts have survived they are to be found not in the custody of the Church of Ireland but in the great national and university collections in Ireland, Great Britain and continental Europe, for following the dissolution of the monasteries in the sixteenth century the contents of their libraries were widely dispersed. The Church of Ireland, as the legal lineal successor of the Church in Ireland, might have been expected to have inherited many of these treasures but, for the most part, this was not the case. The reformed Church of Ireland was puritan in outlook and cared little for such things, and even those items, which by default, remained in the Church's custody or subsequently came into its possession were largely alienated in later centuries. For example, Henry Jones (bishop of Meath, 1661–82) removed the Book of Kells from Kells in 1653 and donated it to Trinity College, Dublin, while in 1854 Lord John George Beresford (archbishop of Armagh, 1822–62) gave the Book of Armagh to the college.[3]

The idyllic world of the Celtic Church was rudely disturbed by the Viking invasions from the late eighth century, but ironically it was these seemingly iconoclastic incursions that provided the motivation for a reform of the Irish Church in the twelfth century that would bring its administration more into line with the western European model. The subsequent settlement of the Danes in Ireland in the eleventh century and their conversion to Christianity, most probably by missionaries from Scandavanian Britain, led to the appointment of bishops in Dublin, Waterford and Limerick who were subject to the authority of Canterbury rather than Armagh. In particular, the consecration in 1106 of Gilbert of Limerick, a close friend of the archbishop of Canterbury, brought the Church into contact with the reform movement in continental Europe which had begun in the monastery of Cluny in France. The first substantial achievement of the reformers was in 1111 when the Synod of Rathbreasil, which was presided over by Bishop Gilbert, divided Ireland into twenty-four dioceses, in addition to the primatial see of Armagh, although the Danish diocese of Dublin was ignored. In 1148 the Synod of Inishpatrick authorized Malachy (archbishop of Armagh, 1132–36; bishop of Down, 1137–48) to travel to Rome to receive the pallium, a vestment which showed that he held his authority from the pope, but he died before reaching Rome. However, in 1152 the pope sent a legate to Ireland to confer pallia on four archbishops – Armagh, Cashel, Tuam and, significantly, Dublin – so completing and regularizing the diocesan administration in Ireland.

---

3 For an overview of Irish medieval manuscripts see the series of Thomas Davis lectures *Great books of Ireland* (Dublin, 1967); Françoise Henry & Genevive Marsh-Micheli, 'Manuscripts and illuminations, 1169–1603' in Art Cosgrove (ed.), *A new history of Ireland ii Medieval Ireland, 1169–1534* (Oxford, 1987), pp 780–815.

One of the consequences of this reform of the diocesan system was a growth in the importance of cathedrals in the life of the Church.[4] The cathedral was the centre of the bishop's administration of his diocese and was the church which contained his throne *(cathedra* in Latin) or official seat. It was usually, although not necessarily, the grandest and most splendid church in the diocese and was initially in the vicinity of the bishop's residence where it was served by the bishop and his household. However, as the bishop's pastoral and administrative duties grew and as worship in the cathedral became more elaborate, responsibility for the administration of the cathedral was gradually delegated to a separate body of clergy. The result was the development of a distinct ecclesiastical corporation, or chapter, with its own rights and privileges. This was usually a secular body of clergy owing allegiance to the bishop and headed by a dean, but it could be a monastic body governed by a prior. In Ireland the development of the cathedral system was essentially a consequence of the Norman invasion. The Celtic Church had not accorded a pre-eminent position to bishops in its polity, and so the churches which held bishops' *cathedra* had not enjoyed a particularly high status. However, during the twelfth and thirteenth centuries existing cathedrals were rebuilt and new edifices erected according to English and continental styles of church architecture. Christ Church cathedral, Dublin, was rebuilt around 1173, probably by masons from the west of England, and similar architectural influences are apparent in the cathedrals of Cashel, Kilkenny and St Patrick's, Dublin, which, together with Kildare, Down, Killaloe, Waterford and Ardfert, were built in the thirteenth century.

Just as England provided the architectural models for Irish cathedrals, so too it provided the administrative model. The clergy who staffed the secular cathedrals were called canons: the word 'canon' originally meant rule, and the cathedral canons at first lived a sort of communal life even though they were not monks. During the Middle Ages the common life was abandoned and the endowments were divided into separate portions to support each member of the chapter. The endowments, which came from the rents, fees and tithes of parishes, were called prebends (from the Latin *praebere* – to supply) because they furnished a living for their holders. The canons came to be called prebendaries and were named after the parish which supported them: for example, the prebendary of Mullabrack in St Patrick's cathedral, Armagh, or the prebendary of Aghour in St Canice's cathedral, Kilkenny.

The chief officer of the cathedral was the dean, who presided over meetings of the chapter. He was, in theory, elected by the chapter, but by the Middle Ages such appointments were usually made on the nomination of the crown. Three other officers, together with the dean, formed the *quatuor personae,* the four cornerstones of the spiritual and temporal life of the cathedral. The precentor was in charge of the services, the music and liturgy, and the choir, while the chancellor kept the cathedral seal, was responsible for education in the cathedral schools, and was usually the librar-

---

4 For a full discussion of the development of cathedral life see Kathleen Edwards, *The English secular cathedrals in the Middle Ages* (2nd ed., Manchester, 1967): S.E. Lemberg, *The reformation of cathedrals: cathedrals in English society, 1485–1603* (Princeton, 1988)

ian and archivist. The treasurer was not, as might be supposed from the title, a financial officer but the guardian of the cathedral treasures – plate, vestments and relics.
Each of these officers had a deputy: the sub-dean, succentor, vice-chancellor and sacrist. The principal function of the cathedral clergy was the *opus Dei,* the daily round
of prayer and praise, with the celebration of the mass, several times each day, as the
central act of worship. As these celebrations became more elaborate they could not
be maintained by the residentiary canons and their places were taken by vicars choral,
that is, deputies (the original meaning of the term 'vicar') who were skilled in singing.
In most cathedrals the vicars choral developed as a separate ecclesiastical corporation
from the dean and chapter and were supported by their own endowments.

All the Irish medieval cathedrals, except two, were secular and conformed (subject to local peculiarities) to the administrative model which has been outlined above.
Christ Church, Dublin, and Down, however, were monastic cathedrals (Augustinian
in the case of the former while Down was a Benedictine foundation) and their
administration differed somewhat from their secular counterparts. Monastic cathedrals were a uniquely English phenomenon (secular arrangements were the norm
in continental Europe) which had developed under the influence of St Dunstan in
the tenth century. A monastic cathedral was headed by a prior. Technically an abbot
was the head of a monastery, but in a monastic cathedral the position of abbot was
held by the bishop who was not usually a monk and so the prior, normally the second in command, was in charge. The prior was aided by assistants called obedien-
taries, the number of whom varied according to the size of the house. The more
important of these were the sub-prior; the sacrist, who had custody of the relics,
vestments and service books; the precentor, who was responsible for the music; the
receiver, who gathered in the revenues from the monastic estates; the cellarer, who
provided food and drink; and the almoner, who distributed relief and looked after
the school for poor boys. These monastic communities were supported by the food
and drink and financial returns from estates which were settled on them by monarchs, nobles and wealthy citizens who were anxious to secure for themselves and
their families the prayers of the community for the repose of their souls.

Like the cathedrals, parishes in Ireland were essentially Norman innovations.
In western Europe the basis of the parochial system was the payment of tithes, a tax
of the tenth part of all the produce of lands, which was due from specific lands for
the support of particular churches, but tithes were not paid in Ireland before the
late twelfth century. The creation of parishes proceeded in Ireland in the late twelfth
and early thirteenth centuries based on Norman manors and, in the areas outside
Norman settlement, on monastic lands or lands of ancient families. By the early
fourteenth century the whole country, with the exception of counties Leitrim and
Longford (the diocese of Ardagh), had a network of parishes, grouped into rural
deaneries which seem to have been based on old Irish territories.[5]

The archives of the medieval church in Ireland – the records of parishes, cathedrals, dioceses and their bishops – have survived only in a fragmentary manner.

5 A.J. Otway-Ruthven, *A history of medieval Ireland* (London, 1968), ch. iv.

2 A page from the churchwardens' accounts of the parish of St Werburgh, Dublin, 1494–6

The unsettled state of medieval Ireland, the dislocating effects of the dissolution of the monasteries and the Reformation, and the periodic unrest to which early modern Ireland was subject were not conditions conducive to the accretion of archival collections.

Only two collections of medieval parish records have survived, these being from the Dublin city churches of St Werburgh and St John. The St Werburgh's material consists of churchwardens' accounts from 1481 to 1520, half a dozen draft leases from the sixteenth century and a parchment folio from a thirteenth-century psalter which, it has been suggested, was used in the church: all of these items are in the Representative Church Body Library.[6] The St John's material is a collection of 203 parish deeds covering the period 1231–1704, of which 156 items pre-date the year 1534: this material is in the Library of Trinity College, Dublin.[7] In addition there are three liturgical manuscripts – two fourteenth-century processionals, one in the Bodleian Library in Oxford and the other in Marsh's Library in Dublin, and a fifteenth-century antiphonary (a book of verses sung by a choir) which is in Trinity.[8] However, the St John's liturgical manuscripts may originally have been acquired for use in Christ Church cathedral, and the close relationship between the cathedral and St John's is in itself a potentially interesting study of the interaction between religious communities in medieval Dublin. The only comparable material which was still extant when inventories of church records were made in the nineteenth century were the medieval deeds of the Dublin city parishes of St Catherine & St James, St Werburgh and St Nicholas Within. These were destroyed in the fire in the Public Record Office of Ireland in 1922. However, one deed from the St Catherine's collection for the year 1309[9] has survived, while the material from the St Catherine's and St Werburgh's collections is available, in part, in published calendars.[10]

Diocesan records have fared somewhat better although there is scarcely an embarrassment of riches. The most important collection, by far, is the seven registers of the archbishops of Armagh, beginning with that of Milo Sweteman in 1361 and ending with that of George Cromer in 1535.[11] Similar registers survive for the dioceses of Dublin (the thirteenth-century Crede Mihi[12] and the sixteenth-century Liber Alani Niger),[13] Ossory (the fourteenth-century Red Book of Ossory)[14] and Limerick (the fourteenth-century Black Book of Limerick).[15] The Armagh registers have been deposited in the Public Record Office in Belfast, the Black Book of Limerick is in the custody of the Roman Catholic diocesan authorities in Limerick, and the other registers are in the Representative Church Body Library. These epis-

6 RCBL, P. 326.   7 Trinity College, Dublin (hereinafter TCD) MS 1477. See also J.L. Robinson, 'On the ancient deeds of the parish of St John, Dublin' in *RIA Proc.*, xxxiii, sect. C, no. 7 (1916), pp 175–224. 8 See William Hawkes, 'The liturgy in Dublin' in *Reportorium Novum*, ii, no. 1 (1957–8), pp 33–67.   9 RCBL P.117.12.1.   10 See H.F. Twiss, 'Some ancient deeds of the parishes of St Catherine and St James, Dublin' in *RIA Proc.*, xxv, sect. C, no. 7 (1919), pp 265–81 & '*Some ancient deeds of the parish of St Werburgh, Dublin*' in *RIA Proc.*, xxv, sect. C, no. 8 (1919), pp 282–315.   11 Public Record Office of Northern Ireland (hereinafter PRONI) DIO4/2/1–13. See also note 62, p. 60 below..   12 RCBL D.6.1. See also note 63, p. 60 below.   13 RCBL D.6.3. See also note 63, p. 60 below.   14 RCBL D.11.1.2. See also note 65, p. 60 below.   15 Limerick Diocesan Archives. See also note 65, p. 60 below.

3 The constitutions of the diocese of Ossory, 1317

copal registers are for the most part compilations of earlier documents, many no longer extant, which affected the rights and privileges of the bishop. They also include contemporary memoranda which would have been necessary for the efficient administration of the diocese: papal bulls and royal grants confirming privileges and possessions; papers relating to appointments, resignations and the discipline of the clergy; leases and related documents concerning estates and advowsons (the right to nominate clergy to a parish). The Liber Alani Niger, for example, was compiled by Archbishop John Alen in the sixteenth century but contains copies of documents from the twelfth century onwards. Also, almost inevitably, diocesan registers contain interpolations of rather more exotic material which has little direct bearing on episcopal administration but which can lend some colour to the interpretation of local events: the Red Book of Ossory, for example, includes the texts of some sixty songs composed in the first half of the fourteenth century by Bishop Richard Ledred for the vicars of St Canice's cathedral to sing at the great festivals so that their mouths 'be not defiled with theatrical, foul and secular songs'. The same volume also includes a treatise on aqua vitae – not, as might be supposed, whiskey, which was not distilled in Ireland until the sixteenth century, but brandy, which in the medieval world was deemed to have medicinal properties.

The profile of cathedral records is even more fragmentary than that of diocesan records. Only two cathedrals, St Patrick's and Christ Church, Dublin, have extant medieval archives. In the case of the former a few pre-Reformation deeds are supplemented by the Dignitas Decani, an early sixteenth-century register containing copies of deeds and related documents from the twelfth century,[16] and by a sixteenth-century account roll. In addition, the Dublin Troper, a fourteenth-century liturgical manuscript, associated with St Patrick's, contains some early sixteenth-century administrative memoranda.[17] The Christ Church material is more extensive but not abundant. There are two surviving registers, the fourteenth-century Liber Niger and the sixteenth-century Liber Albus, which are administrative compilations similar in content to the episcopal registers[18] (that is, copies of documents relating to rights and privileges and contemporary administrative memoranda), fourteenth-century account rolls,[19] some miscellaneous medieval memoranda, and three liturgical manuscripts – a thirteenth-century martyrology, a fourteenth-century psalter[20] and a fifteenth-century book of obits.[21] The last of these, the book of obits, is a particularly valuable source for identifying the members of the cathedral community and those from the wider world who chose to be associated with it. The Christ Church deeds were destroyed in 1922 but they survive in part in an eighteenth-century transcription[22] and as a printed calendar and are an exceedingly rich source of information on people and places from the twelfth century onwards, not only for the cathedral but also for the city and county of Dublin.[23] The medieval

---

16 RCBL C.2.1.1. See also note 69, p. 60 below.   17 Cambridge University Library Add. MS 710. See also note 70, p. 60 below.   18 RCBL C.6.1.1–2. See also note 66, p. 60 below.   19 See note 68, p. 60 below.   20 See Hawkes, 'The liturgy in Dublin'.   21 TCD MS 576.   22 RCBL C.6.1.6.1–3. 23 M.J. McEnery & Raymond Refaussé (eds), *Christ Church deeds* (Dublin, 2000).

muniments of St Patrick's, apart from the Dublin Troper which is in the University Library in Cambridge, are in the Representative Church Body Library, as are those of Christ Church, with the exception of the book of obits and martyrology which are bound together in one volume in Trinity College Library, Dublin, and the psalter, which is in the Bodleian Library.

This small corpus of Irish medieval ecclesiastical archives which has survived may be usefully augmented by the records of the papacy and by the fragmentary administrative records of the Irish religious houses. Since Rome was the spiritual and administrative centre of the western Church, the papal archives inevitably contain much documentation about Irish parishes, dioceses, cathedrals, bishops and clergy with valuable information on the state of the church in localities throughout the country. This is most accessible through the on-going series of *Calendars of papal letters,* amounting so far to nineteen volumes, which covers the years 1198–1513[24] and from *Pontifica Hibernica* which contains papal chancery documents concerning Ireland for the years 640–1261.[25] In addition, registers of a number of Irish monastic foundations survived the dissolution of the monasteries which resulted in the destruction and scattering of the contents of their libraries, cloisters, presses and chests. The extent of the losses, although certainly substantial, cannot be quantified, but a number of these manuscripts did survive: some were secreted and carried abroad into continental Europe, some were retained locally in lay custody, while others were gathered up by intellectuals and collectors such as James Ussher (archbishop of Armagh, 1625–56) whose manuscripts formed the basis of the collection in the Library of Trinity College, Dublin, and Sir James Ware (1594–1666) of Castle Street in Dublin, many of whose manuscripts have ended up in the Bodleian Library in Oxford. In differing ways and at different periods much of this material has found its way into the great public collections of Ireland, Britain and continental Europe; and the riches of the libraries of the Royal Irish Academy, Trinity College, Dublin, the British Library and others are ample testimony to this development.[26]

An invaluable supplement to the limited written record of the Celtic and medieval Church is the evidence of architecture and archaeology. There may be no surviving archives for many of the once important monastic foundations, medieval cathedrals and their satellite churches, but much physical evidence survives, above and below ground, and the work of the national and local heritage bodies has done much in recent years to bring this to light and to interpret it for a wider audience. Publications such as Peter Harbison's monumental work on Irish high crosses,[27] Roger Stalley's seminal study of Cistercian architecture[28] and the survey of the medieval churches of County Offaly[29] provide a wealth of

---

24 *Calendar of entries in the papal registers relating to Great Britain and Ireland,* ed. W.H. Bliss (vols i & ii), W.H. Bliss & C. Johnston (iii), W.H. Bliss & J.A. Twemlow (iv & v), J.A. Twemlow (vi–xiv), M.J. Haren (xv, xviii & xix), A.P. Fuller (xvi) (London & Dublin, 1893–1998). **25** M.P. Sheehy, *Pontifica Hibernica* (2 vols, Dublin, 1962 & 1965). **26** See above, pp 13 & 33. **27** Peter Harbison, *The high crosses of Ireland* (3 vols, Bonn, 1992). **28** Roger Stalley, *The Cistercian monasteries of Ireland* (London & New Haven, 1987). **29** Elizabeth Fitzpatrick & Caimin O'Brien, *The medieval churches of county Offaly* (Dublin, 1998).

information on local sites and buildings, many of which may be visited. Indeed, the portfolio of ecclesiastical buildings in the care of the Office of Public Works, and the accessible literature which is freely available about them, are astonishingly rich sources.

Because so few Irish ecclesiastical records have survived from the medieval period, there is perhaps an understandable reluctance to engage in the study of local medieval ecclesiastical communities for fear that there is little new to discover. However, the Church was involved in virtually all aspects of human activity in medieval Ireland, and so the judicious use of the extant records of central government, municipal corporations and charitable and fraternal bodies, together with the evidence of archaeology and architecture, as supplements to the surviving ecclesiastical sources, offers a prospect of interesting and rewarding research opportunities.

THE CHURCH OF IRELAND 'AS BY LAW ESTABLISHED': FROM THE REFORMATION TO 1871

The Church of Ireland 'as by law established' was a product of the Reformation in the sixteenth century. Following Henry VIII's break with Rome, which was completed in 1534, the Church in Ireland ceased to be part of the universal catholic Church governed from Rome and became an arm of the English establishment in Ireland: in effect a part of the apparatus of government. A parliament of 1536 extended to Ireland the laws governing the Church which had already come into force in England. Thus Henry became the supreme head of the Church of Ireland and all office holders in the Church had to swear to that fact by taking the oath of supremacy. The diocesan or consistorial courts of the bishops continued to exercise a twofold jurisdiction inherited from the medieval Church. The voluntary jurisdiction included the granting of probates and administrations, sequestrations of livings, institutions and collations, licences for marriages, curates and schoolmasters, the granting of faculties for building and alterations to buildings, while the contentious jurisdiction included testamentary and matrimonial suits, tithe cases and causes of correction such as non-residence or immorality by clergy or defamation or adultery by the laity. However, appeals to Rome were forbidden. Yet these reforms had little effect on the day-to-day practice of religion which continued much as before so that the Henrician Reformation was spoken of as having produced 'Catholicism without the Pope'. One aspect of Henry's religious reforms, however, did have a marked effect – the suppression of the monasteries, which began in earnest in 1537. Most religious houses were suppressed and their property, both real and moveable, used to endow the crown and its supporters. Some monasteries were spared and survived in a reformed fashion such as the Benedictine abbey in Downpatrick which became a diocesan cathedral, and the Augustinian foundation of Holy Trinity, Dublin which was transformed into the cathedral of Christ Church with the prior and members of the convent becoming a dean and chapter of secular clergy; other monastic churches such as Inistiogue and St John's, Kilkenny, served as parish churches.

Following the death of Henry VIII and the accession of Edward VI in 1547, the Church of Ireland, in imitation of its English counterpart, began to take on a more protestant character. The principal vehicle for this was the introduction in 1549 of the Book of Common Prayer, which was to be used in all churches throughout the country. This new service book not only provided a reformed liturgy but published it in English; and thereafter English, rather than Latin, gradually became the administrative language of the Church of Ireland. After the brief catholic respite of the reign of Queen Mary (1553–8), Elizabeth I returned the Church of Ireland to protestantism in 1561 with the re-enactment of the Act of Supremacy, by which she became chief governor of the Church, and the imposition of an Act of Uniformity which made compulsory attendance at church services using the Book of Common Prayer.

However, despite the reformation of the Irish Church by the Tudor monarchs, the subsequent plantation of parts of Ireland by English and Scottish settlers, and the effects of the penal laws, the Church of Ireland remained a minority religious denomination; but as the official Church of the State it exercised a degree of influence and wielded an authority which was disproportionate to its numerical strength. Its parishes were units of local government; its courts, centres of matrimonial and testamentary jurisdiction; its prelates and clergy, often important officers of State; and its churches, for periods, the only places in which acts of worship were permitted under the law. The laws which created the established Church were never uniformly applied but were nonetheless of sufficient significance to have created by the middle of the eighteenth century the fabric of the protestant ascendancy. Membership of the established Church was the key not alone to ecclesiastical advancement but to the attainment of public office and the ownership of land. Thus to the ranks of the Church of Ireland were attracted not only those who were convinced by its theology but many who, out of political, social or economic expediency, found it prudent to become, at least nominally, members of the established Church.

The administrative framework of the established Church was in essence not dissimilar to the pre-Reformation Church apart from the substitution of the crown for the pope. It retained, at local level, parishes, dioceses with their bishops and cathedrals, but it was controlled from the centre by the government in the form of the monarch, his ministers and their administrative superstructure.[30] Parish life remained at the heart of the Church, for it was in the local communities that the faithful worshipped, experienced the Christian rites of passage, and ordered much of their social and economic life. The administrative structure of the parish was typically the clergy (a parish priest and perhaps a curate), two churchwardens, a parish clerk, a parish schoolmaster, and the vestries.

30 For a fuller introduction to the administration of the established church see D.H. Akenson, *The Church of Ireland: ecclesiastical reform and revolution, 1800–1885* (New Haven & London, 1971), which, despite its title, provides a useful overview of the eighteenth century.

Then, as today, the clergy were the most important part of the parish administration. They were appointed to their parishes by whoever owned the advowson (the right of presentation to a church living) – usually the bishop or the crown but, in some cases, a prominent local family; for example, the duke of Leinster was patron of the living of Maynooth while the earl of Meath was patron of St Catherine's parish situated in the heart of his family's liberty in Dublin. Clerical incomes came from tithes, fees for pastoral services (baptisms, marriages and burials) and offerings. When the local clergyman was entitled to the whole tithes he was called a 'rector', but the tithes could be acquired by another ecclesiastical person or corporation, a process known as 'appropriation': for example, in the diocese of Cashel the tithes of the parishes Ballydoole, Ballymurreen and Ballysheehan, among others, were appropriated to the vicars choral of Cashel cathedral. Alternatively the tithes could be acquired by a lay person, and this was known as impropriation: for example, the earl of Arran was the impropriator of, *inter alia*, the tithes of Donohill, Dovea and Drom, County Tipperary. In such circumstances the owner of the tithes was obliged to provide a clergyman to fulfill any duties which the owner could not or would not undertake, and such a clergyman was called a 'vicar' (a deputy), who was paid a part of the tithes, the remainder, usually the greater part, being reserved to the owner. The principal duty of the clergy was the cure of souls, which, apart from the celebration of the eucharist and the saying of the offices of morning and evening prayer, was essentially the ordering of baptisms, marriages and burials. The records of this clerical activity are enshrined in the parish registers of baptisms, marriages and burials.

Despite an attempt in 1617 to require clergy to keep registers and to make regular returns to a 'public register' in Dublin, the earliest surviving Church of Ireland register, that for the parish of St John the Evangelist, Dublin, does not begin until 1619. Indeed, until the promulgation of the 1634 Canons of the Irish Church there was no requirement to keep registers, unlike the situation in England where the 1538 Canons had made this obligatory. It is therefore scarcely surprising that only three parishes, all in Dublin (St John, St Bride and St Nicholas Without), are known to have kept registers before 1634. The one supposed fact which almost everyone knows about Church of Ireland parish registers is that they were all destroyed in the fire in the Public Record Office of Ireland in 1922. Like most clichés this is both a simplification and an exaggeration, but it contains a kernel of truth. Records of some 1,006 parishes were destroyed in 1922, but the registers of 637 parishes were at that time held in local custody under retention orders and so survived, while of those registers which were destroyed many had been copied locally in whole or in part before deposit in the Public Record Office. In addition the registers of the important Dublin parishes of St Andrew and St Michan and the mid-seventeenth century register of the Liberties of Cashel had been published by the Parish Register Society of Dublin, and so although the original registers were destroyed in 1922 all the information which they contained has survived.[31]

31 The most recent listing of parish registers is Noel Reid (ed.), *A table of Church of Ireland parochial registers and copies* (Naas, 1994). See note 78, p. 61 below for a list of the publications of the Parish Register Society of Ireland.

4 A page from the register of the parish of St John, Dublin, 1619

[Page   ].

BAPTISMS administered in the Church of _St. Mary's_ in the Parish of _St. Mary's_ in the Diocese of _Connor_ , in the Year 18_91_

When Baptized.	When Born.	Child's Christian Name.	Parents' Name. Christian.	Surname.	Abode.	Quality, Trade, or Profession.	By whom the Ceremony was Performed.
1891 June 10 No.	4 may 1891	Anna	Joseph & Leticia	Cooper	49 Sydney er.	Warehouse	John Spencer
10 June 1891 No.	19 may 1891	James	Thomas & Annie	Gracey	30 Berlin St	Draper	John Spencer
10 June 1891 No.	30 April 1891	John	John & Annie	Barlier	115 Mayo St	Blacker	John Spencer
17 June 1891 No.	27 April 1891	Louisa Jane	George & Eliza	Bennett	37 Lewis St	Sailor	John Spencer
17 June 1891 No.	9 April 1891	Lizzie	James Thomas & Lizzie	McFadden	12 Matchet St	Col. Clerk	John Spencer
17 June 1891 No.	11 April 1891	Roseanne	William John & Roseanne	Patton	Mountain Bush Cave hill Road	Labourer	John Spencer
24 June 1891 No.	14 may 1891	Mary Jane	David Robert & Isabella	Hall	4 Geoffrey St	R.I.C.	John Spencer
24 June 1891 No.	5 June 1891	Thomas	Hugh & Sarah	Glenithen	3 Malcum Place	Carpenter	John Spencer

5 A page from the pro-forma baptismal register of the parish of St Peter, Dublin, 1854

A valuable supplement to parish registers, particularly in parishes for which the registers have been destroyed, are gravestone and memorial inscriptions. Both frequently carry much more information than the names of deceased and the dates of death. Many have details of the extended family and information on places of residence and occupations, while the more florid of them will include appreciations of the character of the deceased. For example, the burial registers of the parish of Drung in County Cavan survive only from 1774 and so do not record the death or burial of one of the parish's most famous sons, Robert Clements, high sheriff of County Cavan, who died in 1722. However, a memorial in the parish church records the event and extols the virtues of one who 'managed the finances of the country and the affairs of his friends with such integrity that no suspicion of dishonesty in them, or of fraud or avarice. could fall upon his name'.[32] In addition to the information which is inscribed on gravestones and memorials, their size, decorative style and location in the church or churchyard may be useful guides to the wealth, sophistication and status of local families. Within the parish church, burial close to the altar was a sure sign of importance in the local community, while in the graveyard a hierarchy of the dead was established by the size of tombs and the prominence of their positions.[33] Inevitably many of the older graveyards are abandoned and overgrown, and their investigation will require an unusual degree of preparation and persistence and a not inconsiderable amount of physical strength to clear undergrowth and, on occasions, to lift up stones which have fallen down. In the case of memorials and gravestones sited within churches, arrangements will have to be made with local custodians since most churches are locked outside the time of services. Although there has not been a systematic programme to record inscriptions, much valuable work has been done and a good deal of this has been published.[34]

In the case of those parish registers which survive, the amount of detail which they contain and, therefore, their usefulness for local studies, varies. The content of seventeenth- and eighteenth-century registers is, for the most part, confined to the date of the event being recorded and the names of the parties involved, with the only general exception to this being baptismal registers which include the names of the parents of the child. In the case of baptismal and burial registers, these are exactly as their title indicates and not records of births and deaths, the dates of which have to be inferred. Burial customarily took place three days after death, but the period between birth and baptism was variable, although, in an age of high infant mortality, the interval was usually a matter of days. Children who were born weak and not expected to live were baptized immediately, usually in private, and, if they survived, were subsequently brought to the parish church to be introduced to the congregation. Baptism, as the Book of Common Prayer required, was a public act, and pri-

32 A.W.P. Malcomson, *Nathaniel Clements: government and the governing elite in Ireland, 1725–75* (Dublin, 2005), p. 14.   **33** For an introduction to the artistic significance of gravestones and memorials see Homan Potterton, *Irish church monuments, 1570–1880* (Belfast, 1985) and Raymond Gillespie, 'Irish funeral monuments and social change, 1500–1700' in S.B. Kennedy & Raymond Gillespie (eds), *Ireland: art into history* (Dublin, 1994).   **34** See p. 62.

vate baptism was reserved for children in a near-death condition or for the offspring of the aristocracy, who were often baptized at home: in both cases, however, the baptism was recorded in the parish register. It is not until the nineteenth century, with the appearance of pro-forma registers, that more detail on individuals and families becomes commonplace – information such as ages, addresses, occupations, dates of birth and death, and often the causes of death. In the case of marriage registers, the inclusion of the names of witnesses, who were frequently members of the family, increases the usefulness of the records while the appearance of signatures allows some conclusions to be drawn about the spread of literacy. Registers can also reflect aspects of the lives of residents of a parish who were not members of the Church of Ireland. Presbyterian ministers were not permitted to conduct marriages until 1782 and could not perform 'mixed marriages' (marriages of a Presbyterian to a non-Presbyterian) before 1845, while Methodists could not conduct marriages until 1845 and did not begin to administer baptism until the 1830s: both denominations resorted to the Church of Ireland for these rites of passage. The same is true of burials, for the Church of Ireland graveyard was frequently used as the burying place for the whole community, including Roman Catholics, although this practice is sometimes obscured by local variants of registration. In some parishes all burials are recorded in the Church of Ireland register and often the religion of the deceased, if not Church of Ireland, is noted, but in other parishes it has been the practice to record only the Church of Ireland interments. However, whilst parish registers are invaluable sources for identifying and analyzing local communities, they are not always a complete chronicle of the community for they are only a record of the three principal Christian rites of passage. It is possible that people lived in a parish for the greater part of their lives and yet did not appear in the register of that parish: they may have been born elsewhere, they may have married, as was the custom from time immemorial, in the parish of the bride, and they may have been buried in a family grave in another part of the country. For a fuller record of the local community, parish registers ought to be used in conjunction with vestry records.

The vestry (its name comes from the word for a room in which the priest kept his vestments and in which the local people met to discuss parish business) was the assembly of all the ratepayers of the parish which, after the abolition of the penal laws, included all ratepayers irrespective of their religion. This, the general vestry (the select vestry, an executive committee of the general vestry, was not introduced until after disestablishment), levied a local tax or cess that paid for a range of services such as street cleaning, poor relief, fire-fighting and policing. The parish cess also funded the maintenance of the parish church, the provision of bread and wine for communion, and the salaries of church servants, such as beadles, vestry clerks and fire-engine keepers, until 1833 when, under the terms of the Irish Church Temporalities Act, responsibility for these matters was passed to central government. The extent of the civil functions which parishes undertook varied from place to place depending on the needs of the local population and the ability of local communities to finance those needs. Inevitably there was more activity in the cities and

At a vestry legally Summon'd and h[...] on Wednesday 1[.]
the 22d. Jan.y 1777 in the parish Church of S.t Nicholas
for said parish. We the Rector, Churchwardens & parish-
...ers do agree that the following Sums of money be raised
and levied on the parishioners of s.d parish for the use of
said Church & Church yard, and for the paym.t of Such
Sums as shall be expended by the present Churchwarden

Sexton's Sallary	£ 10
Sacrament Wine	3.10
D.o Bread	0..9.9
Winding the Clock	5.5
Pen, Ink, paper & making State books	1.2.9
Sand and Brushes	7.9
to the Sexton for washing the Church Linnen	16.3
Visitation fees	6.8
Mr.s B Sutton acc.t	19.10¼
paid for cleaning the pipe of the stoves	1.4
to Mr. Rich.d Rin? for Repairing the Church windows	15
Repairing the Church roof	11.6
Deficiency in the collection appl'd in the 11. Jan.y 1776	3
for a new flew for one of the stoves	3..9
paid for 6 Barrels of coals	1.7
for improvem.t & repairs of the yard	10..19..1
	£38..1..1½

James Norman Alex: Lamilliere, Minister.
                    John Good
            Tho. Alleyn } C. Wardens
                Geo: Fuller
                John Touchstone
                    Will Clark
                Rich.d Burt

larger towns and especially in Dublin where the anglican presence was most per-
vasive. However, the Irish vestries were never as effective as their English counterparts, and many local services were provided on a county basis by the grand juries.
The churchwardens were the principal officers of the general vestry. Two wardens,
who had to be protestants, were elected each year, and their duties were to maintain order during services (the ceremonial wands which churchwardens still carry
have, like civic maces, their origins in the need for a weapon to keep order), to rep-
resent the parish legally and to serve as the parish treasurers.[35]

The records of the vestries are among the richest sources for local and parish
history and for the history of religion in Ireland. Vestry minute books record the
civil and religious activities of the parish, the administrative decisions of the vestry,
and details of those responsible for taking those decisions. The lists of signatures of
those who attended vestry meetings are useful sources for determining places of residence while the records of local services provide much detail, and often much
colour, on the activities of individuals. For example, the records of the watch, an
embryonic police force, in the parish of St John the Evangelist, Dublin, contain
considerable information on local disorder: on Saturday 27 November 1773, Mr
Hassett, 'a Gentleman who belongs to the College as he says' was charged with stab-
bing William Moore, a butcher of Castle Market, while on Tuesday, 1 February
1774, Thomas Whelan and John McDonnough were charged with stealing lead
from the roof of a house in Blind Quay belonging to the lord mayor.[36] Vestry books
may include lists of those who paid the parish cess, and they may contain the annual
financial statements of the churchwardens, although in some parishes there are separate cess books and churchwardens' account books. Cess records are particularly
useful for identifying local communities and estimating the relative status of the
members of a community. They list the names of occupiers of houses in the parish,
street by street, lane by lane, and so can offer, for example, the prospect of exam-
ining shifts in settlement patterns within parishes, while the sums of money for
which each householder was assessed can give an impression of the relative wealth
of individuals and of areas within a town or city.

Relative wealth and status may also be judged by using the records of the allo-
cation of pews in the parish church. Pews were property which could be purchased,
leased or assigned and, like all property rights, it was considered important that they
be recorded lest the benefits of them should be lost or forgotten. These records may
appear in the vestry minute books or in separate pew registers. The most sought-
after pews were those at the front of the church or at the front of the gallery where
the occupants could clearly be seen and from where they would have uninterrupted
views of the sanctuary. The occupation of such pews was a clear statement of status reflecting either newly acquired wealth or longstanding prominence in the community. In many rural parishes the best seats were the preserve of the local landed

---

35 The workings of the Irish vestries have yet to be adequately researched. An introduction to them
may be had from Akenson, *The Church of Ireland* and Virginia Crossman, *Local government in nineteenth
century Ireland* (Belfast, 1994). **36** RCBL P.328.28.3.6.

7 A page from the churchwardens' account of the parish of
St Bride, Dublin, 1690

families, while in Dublin, although the wealthy merchant classes might purchase high-status pews, the best seats in the city were those reserved in St Werburgh's church for the lord lieutenant and his household.

A greater breadth of information may be had from the churchwardens' accounts: expenditure on coal for widows, clothing for poor children and coffins for paupers can reveal much about the charitable dimension of parish life. An examination of the amounts of money spent on bread and wine may allow conclusions to be drawn about the frequency of celebrations of Holy Communion, while the churchwardens' accounts are often prime sources for information on the building, furnishing and maintenance of churches, schools and halls. At best, vestry records are an enormously valuable source of information on clergy, local families and their wealth and status, church buildings and exercise of religion, and what we now think of as local government services. The earliest surviving vestry book is from the parish of St John the Evangelist, Dublin and begins in 1595,[37] while the earliest churchwardens' account book, apart from the medieval accounts of the parish of St Werburgh, Dublin, is from the Dublin parish of St Bride and begins in 1663. However, relatively few parishes have vestry records which pre-date the early years of the eighteenth century.

The value of vestry records as a source for identifying and analyzing local communities is complemented by the records of tithes which, like the parish cess, were a form of tax levied and recorded on a parish basis. Tithes, as a tax on crops, livestock and labour, had been introduced during the reign of Henry II (1154–89) as a means of supporting the Church, but they were not common outside the greater Dublin area until the reign of Elizabeth I (1558–1603) when they became a means of financing the established Church. By the early eighteenth century two-thirds of the Church of Ireland's income came from rectorial tithes. Tithes were payable not only by members of the Church of Ireland but by Roman Catholics and dissenters, and so the records of tithe applotment, or assessment, which were compiled in the 1820s, are invaluable sources not only for estimating the wealth of Church of Ireland communities but also for analyzing the composition of the wider parish. Under the terms of an act of parliament of 1823, tithes could be paid in cash instead of kind, and the sums for which each tithe payer was liable were recorded in the tithe applotment book for each parish. These were compiled by parochial commissioners, one of whom was appointed by the Church of Ireland bishop and the other elected by the ratepayers. The applotment books list not only the payment due to the owner of the tithes, but also the names of the occupiers of land and the quantity and quality of the land they held. Some tithe applotment books have survived among parish record collections in the Representative Church Body Library, but the principal collections are in the National Archives and, for the parishes of Northern Ireland, in the Public Record Office in Belfast. However, in the cities and some larger towns the collection of tithes was not feasible, and the clergy were financed instead by 'ministers' money' which

37 RCBL P.328.5.1; printed in Raymond Gillespie (ed.), *The vestry records of the parish of St John the Evangelist, Dublin, 1595–1658* (Dublin, 2002).

had been authorized by an act of the Irish parliament in 1665 that applied to Dublin, Cork, Limerick, Waterford, Drogheda, Kilkenny, Clonmel and Kinsale. Like the parish cess, ministers' money was payable by all householders, and the amount payable was assessed on the yearly value of property. The records of this tax were often included in the parish cess applotment books or, where there were no separate cess books, in the vestry books. Ministers' money was abolished in 1857, and thereafter the clergy were paid by the Ecclesiastical Commissioners.

Another category of parish record, which, like the tithe applotment books, is nineteenth century in origin, is preachers' books. These volumes record the dates and types of services held in each church, the names of the officiating clergy, the amount of the offertory, the numbers in the congregation and, where appropriate, the numbers receiving Holy Communion. They are, therefore, invaluable records for estimating the health, both financial and spiritual, of a parish and are a useful supplementary source for determining the places in which clergy, particularly curates who might not otherwise be well documented, served. Furthermore they are frequently the only official record of the closure of a church as they record the date of the last service. Preachers' books have been little used by local historians, largely because of doubts about their statistical reliability, and there certainly have been instances in which it has been common practice to estimate, often generously, the size of the congregation rather than count the number of people present. However, preachers' books are often the only guide to the numbers who attended a church and so, despite reservations about their total integrity, they remain an important source for analyzing local Church of Ireland communities. Another aspect of preachers' books, which can provide unexpected local colour and a somewhat capricious range of information and opinion is the comments column. Comments on the weather can often explain variations in church attendance, while the name of a charity or organization for which there was a special service may indicate a particular style of churchmanship or suggest, as in the case of support for overseas missions, an unusual degree of contact between a rural community and the Church in a foreign land. Comments on local events can be valuable as Peter Hart has demonstrated by using preachers' books in County Cork as a source for local outrages during the Civil War of 1922–3,[38] while in a similar vein the comments in the preachers' book of St Stephen's church, Dublin, in Easter Week 1916, provide a vivid impression of activity in the Mount Street area: 'Schools and Parochial Hall seized by the Rebels on Easter Monday 12.30' and on the first Sunday after Easter, 'Fighting very close to the Church during service – 3 bullets hit ch[urch]'.[39] Any appreciation of the value of preachers' books is relatively new. Until recently they were regarded by most parish clergy as being of little significance and were frequently banished to obscure cupboards and out-buildings where their survival was largely a matter of chance. Few such collections, however, fared as disastrously as the preachers' books of one Ulster parish: these for some inexplicable reason were lodged in the boot of the rector's car which was destroyed by fire in a local garage!

38 Peter Hart, *The IRA and its enemies: violence and community in Cork, 1916–1923* (Oxford, 1998).   **39** RCBL P.46.8.17

The nineteenth century, as well as being an era of increasing order in parish administration, was also an age of self-improvement and wholesome recreation, and the parish was often the focus of such activity. Debating societies, drama groups and lawn tennis clubs vied for parishioners' time with Sunday schools, temperance societies, local branches of organizations such as the Young People's Christian Endeavour Society and the YMCA. This activity was resolutely minuted and its costs accounted for, and, although the survival of such records is patchy, they can offer an additional dimension to the study of local Church of Ireland communities.

The survival rate of modern parish records has not been good. Inadequacies in record keeping were commonplace in Ireland; the unsettled state of the country, and in particular the effects of the 1641 Rebellion, the Cromwellian depradations, the Jacobite and Williamite wars and the 1798 Rebellion, militated against the systematic keeping of records, their safe storage and their transmission from one generation to another, while, most catastrophic of all, the fire in the Public Record Office of Ireland in 1922 obliterated the parish collections which had been deposited there. The collections which survive are in the Representative Church Body Library, the National Archives and the Public Record Office in Belfast, although a significant number of parishes still retain custody of their own records.

Above the parishes in the pyramidal structure of the Church of Ireland were the dioceses. In the established Church the diocesan administration was, to all intents and purposes, the bishop and the officers whom he appointed to assist him in his administrative functions. Bishops were appointed by the crown and were, in effect, agents of the English administration in Ireland: therefore they were, for the most part, Englishmen or Irishmen who were sympathetic to the English interest in Ireland. Inevitably also the appointment of bishops was coloured by the current state of English politics, and there was much letter writing and visits to London or Bath, a favourite watering spot for the aristocracy and gentry, when there were episcopal vacancies. For most of the period of the established Church there were four archbishoprics and twenty-two bishoprics. Of course, some were more sought after than others, in particular the archbishoprics of Armagh, Dublin, Cashel and Tuam, in that order, and the bishopric of Derry, and there were frequent translations (that is, internal promotions of bishops) as the holders of Irish bishoprics sought a more prestigious and better-endowed appointment. That is not to say that all the Irish bishops were cynical place-seekers (although many were), but in an age when there was no clear distinction between civil and religious order, patronage and factionalism were accepted aspects of the system.

Episcopal correspondence has tended to be treated as the private property of bishops rather than church archives, and many collections are to be found in national and local repositories in Britain and Ireland rather than among the diocesan archives. Since many of the bishops were English, their correspondence is often to be found among the papers of their families in county record offices or the British Library. For example, Charles Broderick, archbishop of Cashel from 1801 to 1822, was a member of the Midleton family, and his papers are with those of the earls of

Midleton in Surrey County Record Office, while William Stuart, archbishop of Armagh from 1800 to 1822, was the son of the earl of Bute, and his correspondence is to be found with that of his family in the Bedfordshire Record Office. Those collections which remained in Ireland tended to gravitate towards the Library of Trinity College, Dublin, since the Church of Ireland did not have its own library until the 1930s,[40] but for many of the bishops no personal archive is known to survive in any repository, which is scarcely surprising since many were far from distinguished. However, even if many bishops did not generate or preserve their own archive, something of their activity at a diocesan or national level may often be discerned from the national political and religious collections in England. Church of Ireland bishops were part of the English administration in Ireland and so were frequently written to by government ministers and their functionaries in London, and these transactions are preserved in the National Archives in London, in the State Papers, Ireland, and the Home Office Papers, Ireland, series.[41] Furthermore, the Irish bishops and especially the archbishops corresponded with their counterparts in England, and the archives of the archbishops of Canterbury, in Lambeth Palace Library, London, and, to a lesser extent, those of the archbishops of York, in the Borthwick Institute of Historical Research in York, may be useful sources.

The principal functions of the bishops were to ordain and confirm and to visit their dioceses. In fulfilment of these duties they appointed clergy and parish officers whom they could discipline through their diocesan courts. The ordinations of clergy and the licences of parish officers were entered on subscription rolls. These rolls of parchment recorded the nature and date of the offices, included the signatures of the appointees and were prefaced by the subscriptions or oaths which the appointees made: they subscribed to the Act of Supremacy, the Act of Uniformity and declared their opposition to transubstantiation. Appointments of clergy to parishes and the licencing of curates and parishes officers were recorded in diocesan registers (sometimes called 'title books') which also included records of other episcopal acts such as the consecration of a new church or graveyard. Potentially the most labour intensive episcopal activity was visitation, when the diocesan cathedral and all the parishes in the diocese would be inspected by the bishop to determine the physical condition of the buildings, the effectiveness of the clergy and the fidelity of the laity. In well-run dioceses this was a frequent event, and the visitation books which resulted therefrom provide invaluable snapshots of the diocese at particular times. Bishop Isaac Mann's visitation of the diocese of Cork in 1781 recorded the names of the benefices and the clergy (rectors, vicars and curates) who served them, and where they resided; the physical condition of the churches; the size of the glebe; the name of the patron of the living, and the names of the parish clerks, schoolmasters, churchwardens and sidesmen. He noted, among other things, that Templemichael church was in ruins, while in Cork the church of St Paul was in repair but the walls of St Peter's were in danger of falling in, and the rector of

40 See pp 65–6, below.   **41** The State Papers, Ireland and Home Office Papers, Ireland (National Library of Ireland microfilm collection).

Leighmoney was found to have lived four miles away in Bandon while his counterpart in Inchigeelagh was only one of six parochial clergy to reside in a glebe house.[42] Not every function was carried out by the bishop personally: the vicar-general acted as a surrogate or deputy and frequently took the place of the bishop at visitations, in signing licences and in presiding at the diocesan court in which wills were proved, marriage licences issued, and clergy and laity disciplined. In addition the diocesan registrar prepared documents, was in charge of the registry and, in effect, served as the diocesan archivist.

In the registry, as well as the subscription rolls, title books and visitation returns, were the records of the consistorial court, especially probated wills, administrations of estates of those who had died intestate (that is, persons who had not made a will prior to death), marriage licences and marriage licence bonds, and papers relating to disciplinary procedures, particularly against clergy. Following the Henrician Reformation, appeals to Rome were forbidden and jurisdiction in such matters was transferred to the prerogative court of the archbishop of Canterbury and, during the reign of Elizabeth I, these responsibilities were vested in the prerogative court of the archbishop of Armagh which met in Dublin. Similar courts operated at diocesan level with each bishop presiding in person or by surrogate in his consistorial court. Wills were proved and estates administered in the appropriate diocesan court unless the estate of the deceased had a value of £5 or more in another diocese, in which case probate or administration was granted by the prerogative court. In consequence of this activity a huge body of testamentary material of value to historians and genealogists accumulated in the diocesan registries. In particular, the collections of wills and administrations contained much detail about local families and their wealth and property and, in the cases of wills which were proved in the prerogative court, their relationships with the wider world. In 1858 the Probate Act removed this testamentary jurisdiction from the Church of Ireland, and the wills which had been filed in the consistorial courts were transferred to the Public Record Office of Ireland where they were largely destroyed by fire in 1922.[43] However, a considerable amount of the information which was lost in 1922 has survived in printed form[44] or has been recovered from the collections of families, solicitors and genealogists.[45]

Matrimonial jurisdiction was also exercised by the diocesan courts, for until the late-eighteenth century a marriage had to be conducted by Church of Ireland clergy in order to be legally valid. Those intending to marry in the Church of Ireland had first to 'call the banns' in the parish churches of those who were to be married.[46] These announcements provided an opportunity for those who believed the intended marriage to be unlawful to object. An alternative method of proceeding was to obtain a marriage licence from the bishop, but this option also involved indemni-

42 RCBL D.12. 43 For a fuller discussion of testamentary records, see Rosemary ffolliott and Eileen O'Byrne, 'Wills and administrations' in D.F. Begley (ed.), *Irish genealogy: a record finder* (Dublin, 1981) pp 157–80. 44 See pp 52–3. 45 See note 22, p. 55 below. 46 Records of banns, either in the form of separate registers or as part of a parish register of baptisms, marriages and burials, are usually found among parish record collections. However, they rarely pre-date the nineteenth century.

fying the diocesan authorities, by means of a marriage licence bond, against prose-
cution for authorizing an invalid marriage. Matrimonial disputes also came before
the consistorial courts, and the records of such disputes, together with the licences
and bonds, formed an immensely important archive of information on local families and their interaction with families outside their dioceses. As a consequence of
the disestablishment of the Church of Ireland the Church's matrimonial jurisdiction was abolished and its matrimonial records transferred to the Public Record
Office of Ireland where, like the testamentary records, they were largely destroyed
in 1922. However, indexes to marriage licence bonds and some abstracts[47] have survived, and a number of these have been published.[48]

The scenario is similar with matters of discipline. The records of the ecclesiastical courts were also destroyed in 1922, and the fragmentary material which has
survived by way of stray records and abstracts[49] can only hint at the wealth of information, much of it intensely local in its orientation, that was lost. For example, a
series of depositions in the case against Thomas Ward (dean of Connor, 1679–94),
who was deprived of his office for adultery, drunkenness and non-residence, provides graphic evidence of local life from every day people in Carrickfergus and
Lisburn, County Antrim, in the late seventeenth century.[50]

The same is also broadly true of the records of the episcopal estates, which likewise were stored in the diocesan registries. The activities of the bishops were largely
funded by the returns from landed estates, which were part of the diocesan endow-
ment, and their administration produced maps, rentals, rent rolls and tithe records.
These archives not only reflected aspects of episcopal organization but also detailed
much of the lives of the bishops' tenants at different levels of society. The surviving maps of the estates of the archbishops of Dublin, for example, provide a wealth
of information on the tenants and properties of the archbishops and also on adja-
cent landholdings. These estates were located not only, as might be supposed, in
the city and county of Dublin, but also in counties Wicklow, Westmeath and even
Cork for which there is a splendid map of Sherkin Island. Dublin apart, only the
diocese of Armagh has a significant extant estate collection, although there are fragmentary survivals for Ossory, Killaloe, and Cloyne. However, the records in the
Registry of Deeds, Dublin, in which land transactions from 1708 are registered, and
the private papers of families who were episcopal tenants, allow the recovery of the
some information on episcopal estates.

The other part of the diocesan hierarchy was the cathedral, in which the bishop
had his throne and in which, by tradition, he preached and celebrated the eucharist
at Christmas and Easter. Following the Henrician Reformation all cathedrals became
ecclesiastical corporations of secular clergy, that is, they were separate entities under
the law and able to hold property in common for a particular purpose, with a typ-
ical cathedral chapter consisting of a dean, precentor, chancellor, treasurer and a

47 See below p. 58.   **48** See note 26, p. 56 below.   **49** R.J. Hayes (ed.), *Manuscripts sources for the history of Irish civilization* (12 vols, Boston, 1964) and *Manuscript sources for the history of Irish civilization: first
supplement, 1965–1975* (3 vols, Boston, 1979) is still the best guide to such material.   **50** RCBL MS 566.

... Pease for keeping the organs ___ ___   02   00 00
To the Beadle a yeares sallary & Lodging ___ 03   00 00
To the Scavinger a yeares sallary ___ ___   02   00 00
for Cleaning y^e marble at y^e Comunion table 00   07 06
The Procts Allowance ___ ___ ___ ___   12   00 00
      Totall ordinary Disburs^mts ___ ___   233 09 10

        Extraordinary Disburs^mts
for 2 Doz: of Pruckers ___ ___ ___   00   08 00
for Scouring y^e Branch twice & mending it ___ 00   0? 06
To the Vicars the 1st of Nov: p ordr ___ ___ 01   00 00
To the Upholsteror for the seat of the officer of }
  the Traine ___ ___ ___   } 00 13 06
To A guard on Ald^r Quins Body p ordr ___ ___ 00   06 00
To Darys Slator p bill ___ ___ ___   09   19 06
To two laborers in the Church ___ ___   00   02 00
for silver weights ___ ___ ___   00   06 00
To the Smith p bill ___ ___ ___   01   01 10
To John Powell p bill ___ ___ ___   01   09 03
To the Coroner for inquest in 1671 p ordr ___ 00   13 04
To Noakly Slator p bill ___ ___   0?   00 02
more to him p bill ___ ___ ___   19   01 02
more to him ___ ___ ___ ___   0?   00 00
more to him p bill ___ ___ ___   02   14 03
To the Plumor p bill ___ ___ ___   17   09 0?
for a Gowne for the virgor ___ ___   02 ...

variable number of canons. In addition, the vicars choral, the professional core of the choir, might be a separate ecclesiastical corporation with its own endowments. Furthermore there were a number of functionaries who were employees of the cathedral – organists, vergers, sextons, pew-openers and so on. The work of the cathedral revolved around the sung services (matins and evensong daily and the eucharist on Sundays and on feast days), and this *opus Dei,* and the work of administering and financing it, is reflected in the cathedral archives, which were the responsibility of the chancellor. The meetings of the chapter were recorded by the chapter clerk, often a canon and invariably someone with legal training, in the chapter act books, and the accounts were the responsibility of a proctor who was a member of the chapter elected annually and who produced an annual financial statement to justify his stewardship. The estates, which provided the revenues to maintain the building, the canons, and the administrative staff, were sometimes farmed out to stewards or seneschals who commissioned maps and maintained rentals and rent rolls; the music and the records of choir attendance were usually the responsibility of two of the vicars choral appointed for those purposes. In addition there may be registers of baptisms, marriages and burials; building records and architectural drawings; deeds and lease books which can, on occasion, usefully complement the principal series of documents in the cathedral archives.

The diocesan structures outlined above are, of course, ideal, and in reality varied greatly throughout the country depending on the strength of the local Church of Ireland community. Furthermore, and more importantly for our immediate purposes, the diocesan and cathedral archives of the Church of Ireland were, as we have seen, decimated by the fire in the Public Record Office of Ireland in 1922. Only the dioceses of Armagh, Dublin (including Glendalough and Kildare which were united to it), Ossory and Tuam have significant pre-disestablishment archives: the Armagh collection is in the Public Record Office in Belfast and the other collections are in the Representative Church Body Library. In the case of cathedrals there are only three substantial collections, namely, those of Christ Church and St Patrick's, Dublin and St Canice's, Kilkenny, although there are fragmentary collections for Cork,[51] Cloyne[52] and Kildare[53] dating from the seventeenth century, all of which are in the Representative Church Body Library.

The situation is somewhat better at the top of the pyramid, for although the records of central government in Ireland were also destroyed in 1922 the administrative records of England have survived, and so among the public records in London there is much to be learnt about the administration of the Church of Ireland by the bishops and the ministers of state acting on behalf of the crown.[54] A particularly important agency of the government in Church affairs was the Board of First Fruits. First fruits or annates were the first year's revenue of a benefice, dignity or bishopric, and before the Henrician Reformation they were remitted to Rome. Thereafter, this tax was paid to the crown but in 1711 it was transferred to a Board

---

51 RCBL C. 20. **52** RCBL C.12. **53** RCBL C.14. **54** See p. 35 above.

of First Fruits in Dublin which was given authority to use the money to buy up impropriations, aid the building and repair of churches, and assist in the purchase and building of glebe houses. This was an initiative that changed the landscape of Ireland, for the availability of funds led to an explosion of church building as churches which had been in ruins were repaired or more often replaced in whole or in part. Many churches bear the tell-tale marks of Board of First Fruits intervention, having retained only a period tower to which has been added a relatively undistinguished barn-like structure in the place of the former nave and transepts. An even more telling hallmark of the work of the Board is the existence of the ruins of a medieval or early modern church close by an eighteenth- or early nineteenth-century Board of First Fruits building. Perhaps the most striking example of this is in Thomastown, County Kilkenny, where the ruin and the replacement are literally side by side. Rather more distinguished was the role of the Board in facilitating the acquisition or commissioning of glebe houses, and thereby many fine eighteenth and nineteenth-century country houses became Church of Ireland rectories. The records of the Board of First Fruits ought to be one of the most important sources for the history of architecture and building in Ireland but, alas, they too perished in 1922. However, a certain amount of the information is available in copy and extract form in different collections, and while Hayes's *Manuscript sources* can assist in identifying some of these sources, a patient trawl through the lists and indexes in the various repositories may be ultimately more rewarding. More conveniently, the entries in Lewis's *Topographical Dictionary*[55] and in the third and fourth report of the Irish Church Temporalities Commissioners[56] frequently cite the amounts of money which the Board made available to individual parishes, by way of grants and loans, to improve churches and encourage the provision of glebe houses.

The prime sources for information on the architectural heritage of the Church of Ireland have not survived well. Most of the building records and architectural drawings of churches and rectories were destroyed in the fire at the Public Record Office in 1922 either because they were among the contents of the diocesan registries or were part of the archives of the Board of First Fruits, Church Temporalities Commissioners or Ecclesiastical Commissioners. Some building accounts do survive among parish and cathedral records: for example, the records of the demolition and re-building of St Werburgh's church, Dublin, in the eighteenth century;[57] the records of the restoration of Kildare cathedral which began in the 1870s;[58] and the drawings of the distinguished architect, William Burges, for the building of St Fin Barre's cathedral in Cork.[59] There are also small collections of architectural drawings (ground plans, sections and, perhaps most usefully of all, elevations) of churches and rectories among some of the surviving diocesan collections, notably a number of fine drawings by John Semple of churches, mostly in the greater Dublin area, in the 1820s and 1830s,[60] and colourful elevations of churches and rectories in

---

55 Samuel Lewis, *A topographical dictionary of Ireland* (2 vols and atlas, London, 1837). 56 See note 74, p. 43 below. 57 RCBL P.325.27.3. 58 RCBL C.14. 59 NUI, Cork, Boole Library. 60 RCBL D.6.

9 Lusk, County Dublin, from John Moland's map of 1716

the west of Ireland.[61] More substantial are three collections of nineteenth-century drawings of churches which have survived among the records of the Representative Church Body and which may have strayed from the collections of the Ecclesiastical Commissioners. Six volumes of drawings by James Pain, architect of the Board of First Fruits and the Ecclesiastical Commissioners for the ecclesiastical province of Cashel, and four volumes of drawings by Joseph Welland, who was similarly employed in the province of Tuam, are complemented by 27 portfolios of miscellaneous drawings by many of the leading Irish architects of the nineteenth century.[62] In addition, the files of the *Irish Builder*, the leading architectural journal of the late nineteenth and early twentieth century, contain many drawings and descriptions of Church of Ireland edifices both in a contemporary and historical context. Those who are interested in the local architectural dimension of the Church of Ireland should also visit the Irish Architectural Archive. The Archive holds a number of important drawings of churches and glebe houses including W.H. Hill's drawings of St Multose's church, Kinsale, and Thomas Cooley's proposal for a church in Kells, County Meath. More extensive are the Archive's photographic records which catalogue not only individual buildings but also streetscapes, many of which no longer survive. For information on those Irish architects who designed the built heritage of the Church of Ireland, the Irish Architectural Archive's bibliographical index of Irish architects is a peerless source containing some 2,500 references to Church of Ireland buildings between the years 1720 and 1940.

A related and equally elusive visual source is maps. Most of the Church of Ireland map collections were destroyed in the fire at the Public Record Office in 1922. There are no comprehensive and authoritative books of maps of the boundaries of the parishes and dioceses, although occasional maps survive among parish and diocesan collections and among the records of the Representative Church Body.

61 RCBL D.5.   **62** See p. 68, below.

However, in recent years some advances have been made towards reconstructing diocesan atlases, the most significant being Edgar Turner's volume of maps of the parishes in the diocese of Connor, the boundaries of which are roughly co-terminus with County Antrim.[63] The most important surviving map collection is that of the estates of the archbishop of Dublin. This relates mostly to lands in the city of Dublin and counties Dublin and Wicklow, although there are some items from counties Cork and Westmeath, and it covers the period 1654 to 1850.[64] There are also useful collections for the dioceses of Armagh and Clogher from the mid-seventeeth century to the early twentieth century,[65] and small miscellaneous collections for Christ Church[66] and St Patrick's cathedrals, Dublin, mostly from the eighteenth and nineteenth centuries.[67]

Finally, some mention should be made of religious censuses which pre-dated or which were independent of the series of national censuses which began in 1821. The first series of these religious censuses were taken in the 1730s and they were continued periodically in the 1740s, 1750s and 1760s.[68] The best known of these was the 1766 religious census which, at its best, listed the householders in each parish and indicated if they were protestant or papist. This census, like its predecessors, was destroyed in the fire at the Public Record Office of Ireland in 1922, but much of it has survived as transcripts and abstracts: for example the Representative Church Body Library holds transcripts, made by the well-known record agent, Tenison Groves, for a number of parishes in Ulster, Leinster and Munster,[69] while the census for the parish of Aghold, County Carlow, has been preserved in the vestry minute book[70] and that of Navan among the Meath diocesan records.[71] Other censuses were made at local level. Most comprehensive, perhaps, is Bishop Edward Synge's census of the diocese of Elphin which was taken in 1749,[72] while on a more modest level the Revd James Elliott, curate of Scarva in County Down, made several censuses of his parish in the mid-nineteenth century: that of 1851 provided information on name, denomination, ability at school, whether confirmed or a communicant, whether family prayers were said, possession of a bible and prayer book, occupation.[73]

The structure of the established Church survived, largely intact, until the early nineteenth century when, in the face of changing attitudes in Irish society, the Church of Ireland also had to change. The abolition of the penal laws in the late eighteenth century and the winning of Catholic emancipation in 1829 forced on the government the realization that the privileged position enjoyed by the Church of Ireland as the Church of only one eighth of the population could not be sustained. A Church Temporalities Act of 1833 abolished the archbishoprics of Cashel and Tuam, suppressed ten other bishoprics, and replaced the Board of First Fruits with the Ecclesiastical Commissioners who were charged with using the money

63 A copy has been deposited in the Representative Church Body Library. **64** RCBL D.6. **65** PRONI DIO4/22. **66** RCBL C.6.3. **67** RCBL C.2. **68** Brian Gurrin, *Pre-census sources for Irish demography* (Dublin, 2002), pp 44–55. **69** RCBL MSS 23 & 37. **70** RCBL P.522.5.1 **71** Brian Gurrin, 'The union of Navan in 1766' in *Riocht na Midhe*, xiv (2003), pp 144–69. **72** Marie-Louise Legg (ed.), *The census of Elphin, 1749* (Dublin, 2005). **73** RCBL MS 65.

saved by these reforms to build and repair churches and improve the income of clergy in small parishes. The work of the Church Temporalities Commissioners is enshrined in four printed government reports which provide much valuable detail on the state of the Church of Ireland at parish and diocesan level in the early nineteenth century. The first report deals with the revenues and patronage of the bishops and includes the names of the lessees and tenants on the episcopal estates; the second is a similar digest of information for the deans, dignitaries and vicars choral and minor canons of cathedrals; whilst the third and fourth reports provide a mass of detail on parishes – their patrons, clergy, officers, population, extent, churches, rectories, glebe lands, and income.[74] Many of the archives of the Church Temporalties Commissioners and the Ecclesiastical Commissioners were destroyed in 1922 but much remains in the National Archives, the Public Record Office of Northern Ireland and the Representative Church Body Library.

The Irish Church Temporalities Act was a watershed in the administrative history of the Church of Ireland for it was the first time that government had intervened so directly in the affairs of the established Church. Its repercussions were felt both in England, where reaction to the act was the catalyst which led to the emergence of the Oxford Movement, and in Ireland where once the force of reform had gathered pace it could not be stopped. In 1838 the hated tithes were all but abolished; in 1845 civil registration of protestant marriages was introduced by which the Church of Ireland became simply a registration agent for the State with the registers supplied by the government and their contents collated in the General Register Office in Dublin; in 1857 the Probate Act removed the testamentary jurisdiction of church courts and transferred the collections of wills, probates and administrations to the Court of Probate; in 1864 the parish cess was abolished. More importantly, however, the stage was set for the complete severing of the links between Church and State by the disestablishment of the Church of Ireland.

THE CHURCH OF IRELAND AS A VOLUNTARY CHRISTIAN
COMMUNITY: FROM 1871 TO THE PRESENT

The Church of Ireland was disestablished by the Irish Church Act of 1869 which came into force on 1 January 1871. Under the terms of the act the Church was left with the cathedrals, churches and schools then in use, but all other church lands and properties were vested in the Church Temporalities Commissioners who realized these assets and distributed the money to charitable and educational bodies including Maynooth College and the Presbyterian Church. The Church of Ireland was left with the clergy and bishops and a sum of about eight million pounds to fund them, and was free to establish such structures as it thought appropriate for its new condition.[75]

---

74 *First report of His Majesty's commissioners on ecclesiastical revenue and patronage, Ireland* (1814); *Second report* ... (1835); *Third report* ... (1836); *Fourth report* ... (1838). **75** The best guide to the administration of the disestablished Church is J.L.B. Deane, *Church of Ireland handbook* (2nd ed., Dublin, 1982).

The administrative structures which it devised were representative in nature and parliamentary in style. A General Synod was created which would be the Church's parliament and in which supreme authority would reside. Its membership was composed of two houses: the House of Bishops and the House of Representatives, the latter consisting of clergy and laity from each of the dioceses with two lay members for each cleric. The members of the House of Representatives were elected by diocesan synods, which were local versions of the General Synod, and the members of the diocesan synods were elected by the parish vestries. The General Synod met annually, and a Standing Committee, composed of the bishops and two lay and two clerical members from each diocese, conducted business during the year. A similar system obtained in the dioceses with the diocesan synod being an annual assembly and a diocesan council conducting the business throughout the year. The administration of the temporalities of the disestablished Church was the function of the Representative Church Body which was created by the Irish Church Act as a perpetual trustee to take over such money and real and moveable property as were left with the Church of Ireland. It too, as its name implies, was representative in composition, with the bishops being joined by one cleric and two laymen from each diocese.

Apart from the creation of the General Synod, its diocesan equivalents and the Representative Church Body, the administrative apparatus of the Church seemed little changed by disestablishment. The parishes (apart from the introduction of select vestries, executive committees of the general vestries, charged with responsibility for finance, fabric and furnishings) and the dioceses continued to be the principal administrative units and the bishops remained an elite cadre of administrative officers. But if the structures remained much the same, the way in which they worked changed, for a key component of disestablishment was the introduction of the idea of accountability, even if it was not overtly expressed. For the first time in its history the administration of the Church of Ireland from parish level up to the General Synod was accountable to the wider Church through the process of election. In the parishes the select vestries were elected each year, while members of diocesan synods and councils, the General Synod and the Representative Church Body were elected triennielly. Another manifestation of this process of accountability was the production of annual reports by the principal administrative bodies of the Church, at central and local level, and by the host of sub-committees and fixed-term commissions to examine particular issues, which they spawned. The model for this reporting procedure was the *Journal of the General Synod* which was not, as the title might suggest, simply the minutes of the annual meeting of the Synod, although it was that, but more importantly it was also a collection of reports from the various committees and commissions of the Church on their work over the preceeding year. The first General Synod *Journal* appeared in 1871 and has been published annually ever since and ought to be the starting point for any examination of the disestablished Church of Ireland. Similar annual reports were produced at diocesan and parish level and are usually to be found among the diocesan and parish archives.

However, like most annual reports the *Journal* and its local equivalents are digests of information, and the serious researcher will find only a part of the truth therein. The records of the parishes, cathedrals and dioceses continue to be important archival sources for the history of the Church, as do those concerning the activities of the clergy and the bishops. The clergy, of course, were absolved from the post-disestablishment idea of election and, by extension, did not have to report on their activities, but they were responsible to their bishops, who could discipline them if appropriate through the diocesan courts or the Court of the General Synod which replaced the Prerogative Court of the Archbishop of Armagh.[76] The bishops, however, although elected, initially by diocesan synods and more recently by electoral colleges, remained unaccountable and have steadfastly refused to become so. Despite their corporate identity as a house of the General Synod and their propensity to meet regularly, they do not report to the General Synod on their activities. Moreover, unlike the clergy and laity who vote in public at the Synod, the bishops have retained their right to vote in private.

The major archival consequence of disestablishment was the decimation of the archives of the Church of Ireland. As a result of the Irish Church Act the records of the Church, which had hitherto been part of the establishment and, in effect, public records, became the property of a private organization. Concern arose about, in particular, the safety of parish registers, which for the period before civil registration of births, marriages and deaths,[77] were the official records of such activity. The concern was not altruistic but arose from the need to protect information which was essential to establish family relationships and which therefore could affect rights of inheritance. The government legislated in 1875 to bring back into public ownership any Church of Ireland records which related to baptisms, marriages, burials or ordinations, and all such records were to be transferred to the Public Record Office in Dublin. However, this legislation was subsequently amended so that only volumes containing records of baptisms and burials up to the end of 1870 and marriages up to the end of March 1845 came under the terms of the act, and if parishes could show that they could adequately care for their registers (in effect, could store them in a fireproof safe) they were permitted to retain them in local custody. However, despite the amended legislation many parishes, as we have already noted, deposited their registers in the Public Record Office, where they were destroyed in 1922. Since some early parish register volumes also contained vestry minutes, a significant, although largely undocumented, quantity of such records was also lost. The records of the dioceses and cathedrals were similarly affected by disestablishment, as in preparation for the implementation of the Irish Church Act, the Church Temporalities Commissioners largely emptied the diocesan registries and cathedral muniment rooms in their search for evidence of the Church's wealth. When their

---

76 A list of cases which were tried by the Court of the General Synod from 1885 onwards is printed annually in the *Journal of the General Synod*.   **77** Civil registration of protestant marriages began in 1845 and of all births, marriages and deaths in 1864. These records have been collated and indexed in the General Register Office, Dublin.

work was completed, the records were not returned to the Church but were transferred to the Public Record Office with the same catastrophic consequences as for
the parish registers. Furthermore the Irish Church Act ended the residual jurisdiction of the ecclesiastical courts in matrimonial matters and transferred the records
(marriage licences, marriage licence bonds and related material) to the registry of
the Court for Matrimonial Causes from where they passed to the Public Record
Office where they too perished in 1922.[78]

There was, however, a positive side to the events of 1922 since the destruction of so many ecclesiastical archives forced the Church of Ireland, for the first
time, to give some consideration to this aspect of its corporate life. The result was
the creation of an Ecclesiastical Records Committee in 1926 which set out initially
to recover as much as it could of the information which had been lost in 1922.
Copies of and extracts from destroyed records were collected; transcripts, calendars and lists were made of existing records; and from there it was but a short step
to taking custody of archives which could not be adequately cared for in their original parish, cathedral or diocesan custody. Independently of this activity the Church
of Ireland had opened its own library, the Representative Church Body Library,
in 1932 and, in 1939, the functions of the Library and the Ecclesiastical Records
Committee were amalgamated, thereby creating the role of the Representative
Church Body Library as the Church of Ireland's repository for its archives and
manuscripts. As well as providing a home for the archives of the Church of Ireland,
the Library has developed as a focus for the personal papers of clergy and laity and
the records of organizations and societies, dealing with education, mission, charity and recreation, which although closely associated with the Church of Ireland
are not constitutionally part of it.[79]

The loss of many of the Church's archives in 1922 gave an enhanced importance to the work of researchers and scholars who had used these sources before
their destruction. In particular the work of Canon J.B. Leslie and a small number
of contemporaries and predecessors has ensured for posterity an immense body of
biographical information on the clergy.[80] These 'biographical succession lists', as
Leslie termed them, are pen portraits of clergy with details not only of their education and careers but also including, where possible, information on their
antecedents and descendants. Notes of significant events in the life of the parishes
and dioceses in which the clergy served make this an additionally valuable source
for the local researcher. Succession lists were compiled for the clergy of each diocese, and within each volume there are sections on the bishops, cathedral chapters
and parochial clergy with, on occasion, notes on parochial and diocesan history.
Leslie produced succession lists for all the Irish dioceses except Cashel and Emly,[81]

78 Herbert Wood, *A guide to the records deposited in the Public Record Office of Ireland* (Dublin, 1919) is
largely a catalogue of the records which were destroyed in 1922. **79** See pp 69–70 below. **80** See
Raymond Refaussé, 'Church of Ireland clerical succession lists and their compilers' in *Irish Genealogist*,
x, no. 1 (1998), pp 32–41. **81** St J. Seymour, *The succession of parochial clergy in the united dioceses of Cashel
and Emly* (Dublin, 1908).

242   THE IRISH ECCLES

Ecclesiastical Intelligence.

ORDINATION EXAMINATION FOR UNITED DIOCESES OF DOWN AND
CONNOR AND DROMORE.

The Lord Bishop of Down has appointed the following *subjects* of
examination for candidates for Holy Orders in his dioceses. His
lordship would wish it to be understood by them, that, though he
recommends some works under each head, yet if they possess the
requisite information from other sources, he will be satisfied:—

FOR DEACONS.

The Bible.—A sound and accurate knowledge of the Text, including the History and Chronology; the connexion of the Old and New
Testaments in the fulfilment of the Types and Prophecies. Angus's
Introduction to the Study of Sacred Scripture. Graves on the Pen-
tateuch. Davison on Prophecy. Whately (Archbishop) on some
of the Difficulties of St. Paul's Writings. Trench on the Parables.
Wordsworth on "the Canon." Hinds (Bishop) on the Three Tem-
ples. A critical knowledge of the Greek Text of the New Testa-
ment. *The Liturgy and Articles.*—A familiar acquaintance with the
Book of Common Prayer. Wheatley's Illustration of the Book of
Common Prayer. Proctor's History of the Book of Common Prayer.
Cardwell's Conferences (the "Narrative" part). Pearson on the
Creed. Burnet on the Thirty-nine Articles. Davenant, Disputatio
de Justitia (abridged edition). The "Legal and Historical Notes on
the Book of Common Prayer," by Archibald John Stephens, contain
valuable and interesting matter. *Church Government.*—Potter's
Discourse on Church Government (Crosthwaite's edition). *Evidences
of Christianity.*—Paley's Evidence of Christianity. Butler's Analogy.
Ecclesiastical History.—Mosheim's First Five Centuries, and the
Reformation. Short (Bishop) on the History of the Church of
England.   FOR PRIESTS:

As the Bishop considers that the examination of candidates for
Priests' Orders should be more of a *practical* character, he will not
require those who have *already passed* the examination for Deacons'
Orders to be re-examined in the above subjects. The inquiry will
be, if they "have used the office of a deacon well," and are "expert
in the things appertaining to the ecclesiastical administration."
Pastoral Theology.—The preparation and delivery of Sermons and
Lectures; the details of Parochial Visits; management of Sunday
and Daily Schools; Catechising, &c., &c. *Polemics.—The Unita-
rian Controversy:*—Magee on the Atonement. Wardlaw's Discourses
on the Socinian Controversy. *The Romish Controversy:*—Marsh's
Comparative View of the Churches of England and Rome. Taylor's
Dissuasive from Popery (Part I.)

THE HEBREW LANGUAGE—The Bishop gives notice to Candidates for the United Dioceses, that after the Summer ordination of the
year 1859, he will require all candidates for orders to have an accurate knowledge of the Hebrew Grammar; first twelve chapters of
the Book of Genesis; first ten Psalms. Candidates for Deacons'
Orders, whose nomination has been approved by the Bishop, must
forward the following papers to his Chaplain, "Palace, Holywood,"
ten days before the ordination:—University Degree; Divinity Tes-
timonium; Letters Testimonial; Baptismal Certificate; Si quis;
accompanied by a statement of occupation and residence since degree was conferred.

Each candidate for Priests' Orders must produce a private letter
from the incumbent of the parish of which he is curate, stating his
approval of him.   PRESENTATIONS.

FITZGERALD.—Addresses of congratulation on his elevation to
the Episcopal Bench have been presented to the Right Rev. the
Lord Bishop of Cork, Cloyne and Ross, from the clergy of the diocese
of Dublin; from the Dean and Chapter of St. Patrick's Cathedral;
from his former parishioners at Monkstown, Dublin; and from the
Divinity Students of T.C.D., which latter requested that his lordship would publish his course of lectures on Ecclesiastical History.

GALBRAITH.—An address, signed by about 600 of the students of
Trinity College, has been presented to the Rev. Joseph A. Galbraith,
F.T.C.D., congratulating him on his success in defeating the action
recently taken against him for libel.

METGE.—An address, and purse containing 60½ sovereigns, has
been presented to the Rev. William Metge, by the parishioners of
Seapatrick, diocese of Dromore, of which parish he has been curate
for sixteen years.

10 Detail from a page of *Irish Ecclesiastical Gazette*, 1857

Cork, Cloyne and Ross,[82] Dromore,[83] and Waterford and Lismore,[84] for which successions had been published or were under way before he began his work, and whilst
a number of Leslie's lists were printed,[85] many remain unpublished as does his four-
volume index to all the succession lists.[86]

The archives and manuscripts of the Church are complemented by two invaluable primary printed sources, the *Church of Ireland Gazette* and the *Church of Ireland
Directory*. The *Gazette,* which is the longest running weekly church newspaper in
Great Britain and Ireland, began its existence in 1856 as the *Irish Ecclesiastical Gazette*
and changed to its present title in 1900. It is a kaleidoscope of ecclesiastical information containing reports and comments on a wide variety of issues which absorbed
the Church of Ireland, both nationally and locally, publishing the texts of sermons
and addresses, reviewing books, and advertising an astonishing range of activities
and services. Most valuable perhaps for the local historian is the section in each issue,
quaintly entitled 'Ecclesiastical Intelligence' which contained short accounts of local
events in each diocese: the consecration of a church, the appointment of clergy, the
installation of stained glass windows or the erection of memorials. Often the *Gazette*
is the only source for dating such events. There is a complete run of the *Gazette* in
the Representative Church Body Library together with typescript indexes. The
most obvious limitation of the *Gazette* is that it does not begin until 1856. However,
two other publications, the *Christian Examiner,* which began publication in 1825,
and the *Irish Ecclesiastical Journal,* which appeared first in 1840, can provide valuable
snippets of information on local Church of Ireland activity for earlier in the nineteenth century. The *Church of Ireland Directory* began in 1862 as *The Irish Church
Directory* and changed to its present title only in 1967. It provided, for the first time,
an annual list of clergy with information on their university degrees, dates of ordination and institution together with details of the benefices which they held, the
size and value of the glebe, the numbers of worshippers who could be accommo-
dated in the church and the name of the patron of the living. In addition the *Directory*
carried a variety of supplementary details on diocesan officers and on Church of
Ireland schools and voluntary organizations. There had been earlier Church of
Ireland directories but they were occasional publications[87] rather than annuals; more-

---

82 W.M. Brady, *Clerical and parochial records of Cork, Cloyne, and Ross* (Dublin, 1863–4); this was continued as J.H. Cole, *Church and parish records of the united diocese of Cork, Cloyne, and Ross* (Cork, 1903).
83 H.B. Swanzy, *Succession lists of the diocese of Dromore* (Belfast, 1933); an updated edition has been published as *Clergy of Down and Dromore* (Belfast, 1996).   84 W.H. Rennison, *Succession lists of the bishops,
cathedral and parochial clergy of the dioceses of Waterford and Lismore* (Ardmore, 1920).   85 J.B. Leslie, *Armagh
clergy and parishes* (Dundalk, 1911); idem, *Clogher clergy and parishes* (Enniskillen, 1929); idem, *Ossory
clergy and parishes* (Enniskillen, 1933); idem, *Ferns clergy and parishes* (Dublin, 1936); idem, *Derry clergy
and parishes* (Enniskillen, 1937); idem, *Raphoe clergy and parishes* (Enniskillen, 1940); idem, *Supplement
to 'Armagh Clergy & Parishes'* (Dundalk, 1948); J.B. Leslie and H.B. Swanzy, *Biographical succession lists
of the clergy of the diocese of Down* (Enniskillen, 1936); *Clergy of Connor* (Belfast, 1993). Updated editions
have been published as *Clergy of Down and Dromore* (Belfast, 1996), *Clergy of Derry and Raphoe* (Belfast,
1999), W.E.C. Fleming, *Armagh clergy, 1800–2000* (Dundalk, 2001).   86 RCBL MS 61.   87 See S.P.
Lea, *The present state of the established church or ecclesiastical register of Ireland for the year 1814* (Dublin, 1814);

11 Portrait of Richard Chenevix Trench, archbishop of Dublin, 1864–84

over, Irish clergy were not included in that great compendium of British clergy, *Crockford's Clerical Directory,* until 1883.

In 1967 the *Directory* introduced photographs of bishops and if this was the first occasion on which the Church of Ireland officially illustrated its prelates in such a way, it was no more than a public recognition of an activity which had been going on since the late sixteenth century. The acquisition and commissioning of portraits, mainly of bishops, but also in some places of deans, and often from the leading artists of the day, has created a substantial collection of colourful images of the leading churchmen of the last four centuries which are now to be found in episcopal residences, cathedrals and synod halls throughout the country.[88] The development of photography in the nineteenth century allowed the images of lesser clergy to be inexpensively recorded, and many vestries are decorated with photographs of the rectors and curates who served in the parochial ministry. Taken together, the Church's collection of portraits and photographs of bishops and clergy, with their capacity to lend colour, both literally and metaphorically, to local studies, is an enormously valuable resource. Church of Ireland figures, both lay and clerical, were prominent also in the affairs of other leading Irish institutions, and the portrait collections of organizations such as Dublin Corporation, Trinity College, Dublin, and

J.M. Bourns, *The Irish clergy list and ecclesiastical almanack* (Dublin, 1843); *The Irish churchman's almanac* (Belfast, 1855); S.B. Oldham, *The clerical directory for Ireland* (Dublin, 1858). **88** See note 92, on p. 62 below.

the King's Inns are likely to contain useful material as are the more important public gallery collections in Dublin, Belfast and Cork.

Finally, two sources which are neither manuscript nor printed, and which,
because they have been thought of as more decorative than informational, have
been little used – church plate and stained glass windows. Chalices, patens, flagons,
alms dishes, collecting plates, mostly in silver but also in silver gilt and silver plate,
and frequently the work of leading Dublin and provincial silversmiths, were, more
often than not, commemorative pieces. They were given or commissioned to mark
the opening of a new church, to celebrate the fidelity of local clergy, to memori-
alize bishops and clergy, to give thanks for the birth of a child or to remember the
life of a faithful member of a parish. As such they are often inscribed with genealogical and topographical information which can add much to local studies while their
worth as artistic objects and their significance as pieces of church property can tes-
tify eloquently to the wealth, vibrancy and sophistication of local communities and
their leaders. Most of the Church's collection of plate is in regular use and so is scat-
tered in parishes and cathedrals throughout the country and not immediately available to researchers. However, a database in the Representative Church Body Library
holds information on most of the pieces and while there is no public access to it,
written requests for information from this source will be considered.

As with church plate, stained glass windows, too, are frequently memorials and
often the work of celebrated Irish artists of the nineteenth and twentieth centuries.
Windows commemorate local families, faithful clergy, acts of charity, and individuals who have died, often in tragic circumstances. In Arklow, County Wicklow, a
window commemorates Henry Hodgson and his wife, Anne Elizabeth, 'for their
help and work during the Irish famine of 1847', while in Lisburn, County Antrim,
two windows in Christ Church cathedral are memorials to Sir Richard Wallace,
one of the principal benefactors of the town in the nineteenth century. A significant number of windows are war memorials: for example, Michael Healy's mag-
nificent window in Castlecomer parish church, County Kilkenny, is a memorial to
Christopher Butler Prior-Wandesforde, a member of a prominent local family, who
died from his wounds in France in 1917, while in St Nicholas's collegiate church,
Galway, there is a window commemorating the son of the rector, Edward
Fleetwood Berry of the Gurkha Rifles, who was killed in 1916.[89] The stained glass
of the Church of Ireland is currently being surveyed, diocese by diocese, and the
results, to date, are available in the Representative Church Body Library and the
Irish Architectural Archive in hard copy and on a database.

89 I am grateful to the Revd Mark Hayden, Dr David Lawrence and Mrs Lesley Whiteside for advice
on stained glass.

CHAPTER 2

Access to the archives and manuscripts
of the Church of Ireland

INTELLECTUAL ACCESS: HISTORIES, CATALOGUES AND EDITIONS

As in any form of original research, the successful use of Church of Ireland archives and manuscripts in local history projects will be enhanced and the research greatly facilitated by consulting the available printed sources before tackling the manuscript material. All researchers should familiarize themselves with the outline of the history and administration of the Church of Ireland, consult any published catalogues and lists of archives and manuscripts, and, where possible, use published editions of documents in the first instance. Much, if not all of this work can be done in any self-respecting reference library, thus saving time and money that might be involved in travelling to the various repositories in which Church of Ireland material is to be found.

The most accessible history of the Church of Ireland is Kenneth Milne's short history, the most recent edition of which brings the story up to the year 2000.[1] R.B. MacCarthy's history, while equally brief, is somewhat idiosyncratic, although its origins, as a set of lectures given in Kilkenny with local examples, may make it particularly apposite reading for those whose research is centred on that area.[2] The standard academic history remains the three-volume multi-authored study which was edited by Alison Phillips in 1933.[3] However, Milne's history, in particular, provides a balanced and measured overview of the development of the Church of Ireland from St Patrick to the present, and the short time required to read it will equip the researcher with a context in which to better understand the locality in which he or she proposes to work. It might also be useful, although perhaps not essential in the initial stages of research, to look at one of the guides to the administration of the Church. D.H. Akenson's chapter entitled 'The eighteenth century church as an administrative system'[4] is a useful introduction, while for the Church today the most up-to-date work is Deane's *Church of Ireland handbook,* although Gilbert Wilson's earlier work has a helpful administrative chart.[5] Many will find these to be valuable at the beginning of their research, although others may prefer to use them as reference works as they proceed. At a more local level there are a

---

1 Kenneth Milne, *The Church of Ireland: a history* (4th ed., Dublin, 2003). 2 R.B. MacCarthy, *Ancient & modern: a short history of the Church of Ireland* (Dublin, 1995). 3 W.A. Phillips (ed.), *History of the Church of Ireland from the earliest times to the present day* (3 vols, Oxford, 1933). 4 D.H. Akenson, *The Church of Ireland: ecclesiastical reform and revolution, 1800–1885* (New Haven & London, 1971). 5 Deane, *Church of Ireland handbook*; W.G. Wilson, *How the Church of Ireland is governed* (Dublin, 1963).

number of diocesan and cathedral histories and a proliferation of publications relating to individual parishes. These vary considerably in size, scope and quality ranging from brief commemorative booklets to full-scale academic studies. However, even the most limited of them can provide a useful local chronology and context while the best are invaluable sources often containing local information, sometimes from oral sources, which is unavailable elsewhere. Older parish histories, especially those published at the end of the nineteenth century, frequently include long transcripts of parish records, especially protracted extracts from registers and vestry books, and these assume an added significance in the context of parishes for which the records have been destroyed subsequently. The *Irish Builder*[6] likewise included excerpts from parish records: for example, in the volume for 1886 there is an extended history of the parish of St Audoen, Dublin, including lengthy quotations from the vestry minute books, the originals of which have been missing for many years, and a running series on the churches of County Laois. The largest and most accessible collections of Church of Ireland parish histories are in the Representative Church Body Library.[7]

Published calendars, lists, indexes and descriptive articles on Church of Ireland archives and manuscripts do not abound, but if there are relatively few specific publications, enough general catalogues and directories have appeared to give researchers an introduction to the topic with the minimum of effort. Pre-eminent in this regard is the multi-volume *Manuscript sources for the history of Irish civilization* and its three-volume *Supplement*.[8] These comprise brief catalogue entries for archives and manuscripts relating to Ireland which are located in repositories not only in Ireland but throughout the world. The entries are arranged thematically with separate volumes for subjects, dates, places, persons and repositories. As well as describing the material, the catalogue entries include a location guide, which in the case of overseas material is often a reference to a microfilm in the National Library of Ireland whose extensive microfilming programme has made much, otherwise inaccessible material, readily available in Dublin. So, for example, by looking in the subject volume under the heading of visitations, a researcher can easily identify which dioceses have extant visitation books, for which period, and where they may be consulted. On a broader front one can look under the subject of Church of Ireland, which in turn is sub-divided into ten categories (benefices, clergy, controversy, conversions, convocation, disestablishment, liturgy, missions, property and revenue, general and miscellaneous) and obtain an overall impression of the types of manuscript sources which are available.

However, *Manuscript sources* was published in 1965 and the *Supplement* in 1979 and, as much has happened in Church of Ireland archival circles since then, these

6 The *Irish Builder* began as the *Dublin Builder* and changed its title in 1867.   **7** A useful introduction to the published works about the Church of Ireland is Kenneth Milne (ed.), *A Church of Ireland bibliography* (Dublin, 2005). For a comprehensive catalogue of shorter works on Church of Ireland topics see R.J. Hayes (ed.), *Sources for the history of Irish civilization: articles in Irish periodicals* (9 vols, Boston, 1970).   **8** See note 49, p. 37 above.

volumes should be used in conjunction with more recent listings. Such a source is the National Register of Archives, now maintained by the British National Archives in Kew, which each year solicits lists and indexes of archives and manuscripts, both published and unpublished, from British and Irish repositories. A master index allows researchers to discover quickly if there is relevant material among the lists, and this facility is now available on the British National Archives website.[9] The National Library of Ireland, Trinity College, Dublin, the Public Record Office of Northern Ireland and the Representative Church Body Library regularly send material to the National Register, and other Irish repositories have also contributed from time to time. Periodic digests of these contributions are published in *Irish Historical Studies*. However, the National Register operates a cut-off date of 1922 for Irish material and so is of limited significance for those engaged in twentieth-century studies. The National Register of Archives is a part of the Royal Commission on Historical Manuscripts which, since its foundation in 1869, has been surveying important collections of manuscripts and publishing the results of these exercises. Before Irish independence, the writ of the Commission also ran in Ireland, and many important Irish archives, including some Church of Ireland collections, were surveyed. These included the archives of the dioceses of Dublin and Ossory which were described by John Gilbert in the Commission's tenth report[10] and the voluminous correspondence of William King, bishop of Derry and archbishop of Dublin in the late seventeenth and early eighteenth century, an account of which appeared in the second report.[11]

The most complete overview of Irish archival repositories is the *Directory of Irish archives*, which includes brief descriptions of the contents of most Irish repositories, and is a useful introduction to lesser known collections which may contain Church of Ireland material. For example, the entry for the Erasmus Smith Trust reveals that it is an educational foundation which had protestant schools and estates in counties Clare, Dublin, Galway, Tipperary, Limerick, Sligo and Waterford from the seventeenth to the twentieth century.[12] Another useful directory, although more specific in its content, is the *Directory of historic Dublin guilds*,[13] which includes information on sources for trades guilds and religious confraternaties in the capital. The trade guilds controlled local government in Dublin until 1841, and, from the Reformation until the Roman Catholic relief acts of the late eighteenth century, were dominated by members of the established Church. Similar guilds operated in other Irish towns and cities, and their records are invaluable sources for the study of the Church of Ireland in early-modern Ireland, for the organization of trade, and for the development of municipal corporations.[14] Religious confraternities were important social

9 www.nationalarchives.gov.uk 10 J.T. Gilbert, 'Archives of the see of Dublin' & 'Archives of the see of Ossory' in Historical Manuscripts Commission, *Tenth report*, appendix, pt v (London, 1855), pp 204–64. 11 J.T. Gilbert, 'Correspondence and papers of William King, archbishop of Dublin' in Historical Manuscripts Commission, *Second report*, appendix (London, 1874), pp 231–62. 12 Seamus Helferty & Raymond Refaussé (eds), *Directory of Irish archives* (4th ed., Dublin, 2003). 13 Mary Clark & Raymond Refaussé, *Directory of historic Dublin guilds* (Dublin, 1993). 14 For information on the

and religious foci in late medieval and early-modern Ireland. They provided a medium for lay people of modest means to join together to finance the practice of obituarial prayer whereby priests were employed to say mass for the repose of the souls of former members of the confraternity. This activity was generally sited in guild chapels in parish churches and cathedrals. Following the Reformation, which largely ended this obituarial practice, these buildings passed into the custody of the Church of Ireland, and much of the physical and documentary evidence of the life of the religious guilds was absorbed into the established Church. The work of Colm Lennon,[15] in particular, has indicated the importance of the role of the religious confraternities in the social and religious life of Dublin. As in the case of the trades guilds, confraternities existed in other Irish towns and cities although they are less well documented.

A number of Irish repositories have published general catalogues of their manuscript holdings, and some of these contain valuable details of Church of Ireland records. The Library of Trinity College, Dublin, is a particularly rich source, for the College was founded in the late sixteenth century to train Church of Ireland clergy and until relatively recently had a pronounced Church of Ireland ethos. Abbott's *Catalogue of manuscripts*[16] includes brief descriptions of many collections which bear upon the Church of Ireland. There are papers of prominent prelates such as James Ussher (archbishop of Armagh, 1625–56), Jonathan Swift, the eighteenth-century dean of St Patrick's cathedral, Dublin, and Joseph Stock, bishop of Killala during the 1798 Rebellion, along with administrative records like the fifteenth-century register of the court of the archbishop of Dublin containing details of wills, visitations and legal processes. As well there are transcriptions of now destroyed archives such as the royal visitations of the dioceses of the Church of Ireland in the years 1615 and 1633–4. These were copied by William Reeves (bishop of Down and Connor, 1886–92), whose archival and historical skills were so highly regarded that he was offered the post of deputy keeper of the public records in both Ireland and Scotland. Mark Colker's catalogue of Latin and Renaissance manuscripts in Trinity[17] provides fuller descriptions of many items which are summarily noted in Abbott's catalogue, including ecclesiastical manuscripts which have associations with the Church of Ireland. For example, his descriptions of the book of obits of Christ Church cathedral, Dublin and the antiphonary (book of verses sung by a choir) of St John's church, Dublin, are valuable for the interpretation of the membership and the liturgical practices of these late medieval urban religious communities. His identification of the ownership of individual manuscripts often provides interesting sidelights on learning in the mod-

records of guilds and confraternities outside Dublin see Hayes, *Manuscript sources for the history of Irish civilization*, v.   **15** See in particular Colm Lennon, 'The chantries in the Irish Reformation: the case of St Anne's guild, Dublin, 1550–1630' in R.V. Comerford et al. (eds), *Religion, conflict and coexistence in Ireland* (Dublin, 1990); idem, 'The survival of the confraternities in post-Reformation Dublin' in *Confraternitas*, vi, no. 1 (spring 1995), pp 5–12.   **16** T.K. Abbott, *Catalogue of the manuscripts in the Library of Trinity College, Dublin* (Dublin, 1900).   **17** M.L. Colker, *Trinity College Library Dublin: descriptive catalogue of the medieval and renaissance Latin manuscripts* (2 vols, Aldershot, 1991).

ern Church of Ireland – why did Thomas Rundle, the eighteenth-century bishop of Derry, have a manuscript of the works of Plato, and what propelled Henry Jones (bishop of Meath, 1661–82) to remove the Book of Kells from the local parish church and present it to Trinity College?

To a lesser extent, categories of material similar to those in Trinity appear in the catalogue of manuscripts of the Gilbert Library, now part of Dublin City Library and Archive:[18] correspondence of bishops such as Thomas Otway, bishop of Ossory in the late seventeenth century, and William Nicholson (bishop of Derry, 1718–27); drawings and engravings of monuments in Dublin churches; and, perhaps more surprisingly, correspondence of the Cork antiquarian, Richard Caulfield (1823–87), much of it with Church of Ireland clergy who had an historical bent, relating to archaeological and historical matters in the south-west of Ireland in general and County Cork in particular in the middle years of the nineteenth century.

More recently published is a *Guide to the archives of the Office of Public Works*.[19] This is a useful introduction for those who are interested in church properties which had belonged to the established Church of Ireland but which subsequently became the property of the State – major ecclesiastical settlements such as Clonmacnoise, Glendalough and the Rock of Cashel and less well-known church sites like Ardmore, County Waterford, and Kilcullen, County Kildare.

There is, regrettably, no comprehensive modern guide to the holdings of the National Archives in Dublin.[20] Herbert Wood's guide to the Public Record Office of Ireland is largely a catalogue of the records which were destroyed in the Four Courts fire in 1922, and although the post-1922 situation is interpreted to some extent by Margaret Griffith's subsequent short guide,[21] this is a very brief introduction to the principal record office of the Irish State. However, the sections on parochial records and, in particular, that on non-official material are useful. The former lists those parishes for which copies of registers, in whole or in part survive, while the latter provides references to a number of local collections such as the records of the civil administration of the parish of St Thomas, Dublin, which encompassed Luke Gardiner's fashionable eighteenth-century development of Rutland Square and Sackville Mall, and the Revd William Henry's description of counties Sligo, Donegal and Fermanagh in 1739. In addition to the short guide, the 55th to the 59th *Reports of the deputy keeper of the public records in Ireland* include summaries of accessions from 1922 to 1961 while *Sources for local studies in the Public Record Office of Ireland*[22] has sections on parish registers and tithe applotment books. As in Dublin, so too in Belfast there is no comprehensive guide or catalogue to the holdings of the Public Record Office of Northern Ireland which would allow researchers to

---

18 Douglas Hyde and D.J. O'Donoghue (comps), *Catalogue of the books and manuscripts comprising of the library of the late Sir John T. Gilbert* (Dublin, 1918). **19** Rena Lohan, *Guide to the archives of the Office of Public Works* (Dublin, 1994). **20** The Public Record Office of Ireland and the State Paper Office were amalgamated in 1986 to form the National Archives. **21** Margaret Griffith, 'A short guide to the Public Record Office of Ireland' in *Irish Historical Studies*, viii, no. 29 (Mar. 1952), pp 45–58. A revised version of this article was published in pamphlet form in 1964. **22** *Sources for local studies in the Public Record Office of Ireland* (Dublin, 1982).

identify at a distance the various categories of Church of Ireland material held there. However, the Belfast Record Office has conscientiously published its deputy keeper's reports from 1921 to 1989 and an annual report from 1990, all of which give helpful information on accessions. In addition, its *Guide to church records*[23] includes listings of all Church of Ireland parish records, in original or copy form, which are available there.

Like the National Archives and the Public Record Office of Northern Ireland, the Representative Church Body Library, which is the Church of Ireland's principal repository for its archives and manuscripts, does not have a modern printed catalogue. J.B. Leslie's *Catalogue of manuscripts*[24] was published in 1938, before the Library as an archival repository had been established, and although it lists, in brief, material which is still in the collection of the Representative Church Body Library, it also includes references to archives and manuscripts which are no longer present. It is, in short, seriously out of date and therefore more likely to confuse than enlighten researchers. However, although Leslie's *Catalogue* has not yet been replaced, there have been a number of more recent descriptive articles on the Library's holdings. Geraldine Fitzgerald's article in *Analecta Hibernica* on 'Manuscripts in the Representative Church Body Library'[25] was followed in the 1980s and 1990s by a series of pieces in genealogical, archival and historical journals: lists and indexes of the Swanzy pedigree notebooks, which relate largely to families in north-east Ulster; the pedigrees, wills and miscellaneous gleanings of the Cork genealogist, W.H. Welply; T.U. Sadlier's copies of marriage licences from the dioceses of Ossory;[26] descriptions of collections such as the diocesan records of Cloyne[27] and the muniments of Christ Church cathedral, Dublin;[28] and general overviews of the collection like those which appeared in *Irish Archives Bulletin, Saothar,* and *Archivium Hibernicum.*[29] In addition, handlists of holdings of parish registers and vestry minute books, arranged on a county basis, are regularly produced by the Library and annual accessions lists have been printed in *Journal of the General Synod* since 1928.

Some of the other Church of Ireland repositories (diocesan, cathedral and 'public' libraries) have from time to time published brief catalogues of their contents,

23 *An Irish genealogical source. Guide to church records* (Belfast, 1993). **24** J.B. Leslie, *Catalogue of manuscripts in possession of the Representative Church Body ... collected by the Ecclesiastical Records Committee* (Dublin, 1938) **25** Geraldine Fitzgerald, 'Manuscripts in the Representative Church Body Library' in *Analecta Hibernica*, no. 23 (1966), pp 307–9. **26** Raymond Refaussé, 'The Swanzy pedigree notebooks in the Representative Church Body Library' in *Irish Genealogist*, vi, no. 4 (1983) pp 526–9; idem, 'The Welply will abstracts' in *Irish Genealogist*, vi, no. 6 (1985), pp 814–23 & vii, no. 1 (1986), pp 113–21; idem, 'W.H. Welply's pedigree notebooks' in *Irish Genealogist*, vii, no. 3 (1987), pp 421–32; idem, 'Marriage licences from the Diocese of Ossory, 1739–1804' in *Irish Genealogist*, vii, nos 1–3 (1990–92), pp 122–44, 239–67, 393–428. **27** Susan Hood, 'The diocesan records of Cloyne, County Cork' in *Irish Genealogist*, ix, no. 4 (1997), pp 426–37. **28** Raymond Gillespie, 'The archives of Christ Church cathedral, Dublin' in *Irish Archives*, v, no. 2 (1998), pp 3–11. **29** Raymond Refaussé, 'The archives of the Church of Ireland: an introduction' in *Irish Archives Bulletin*, xi (1981), pp 3–11; idem, 'Sources for labour history in the Representative Church Body Library, Dublin' in *Saothar*, no. 20 (1995), pp 95–6; idem, 'The archives of the Church of Ireland and the Representative Church Body Library' in *Archivium Hibernicum*, xlix (1995), pp 115–24.

and whilst most of these are now rather dated, yet, in the absence of more modern listings, they can still prove useful.[30] The most substantial of these is Newport White's catalogue of the manuscripts in Marsh's Library, Dublin,[31] which includes materials from the libraries of Archbishop Narcissus Marsh, John Sterne (bishop of Clogher, 1717–45) and the jurist, Dudley Loftus. The collection is very miscellaneous but contains many items which might illuminate local studies: for example, memorials and letters relating to a dispute in 1781 between the bishop of Down and Connor, Edward Smith, and James Bell, a dissenter who refused to act as a churchwarden, and an early eighteenth-century commission to value the improvements made by Alexander Cairncross, bishop of Raphoe, to his see in County Donegal. Marsh's Library was incorporated in 1707 as the first public library in Ireland, and later in the century, in 1773, a similar library was established in Armagh by the then archbishop of Armagh, Richard Robinson. This library also has a manuscript collection of which there is a short printed catalogue.[32] Inevitably it contains much about Armagh (the cathedral, city and diocese), about the diocese of Clogher which was united to Armagh from 1850 to 1856, and about the administration of the diocese of Meath, which was the senior bishopric in the province of Armagh, particularly during the episcopate of Anthony Dopping in the late seventeenth century. Less predictable is the presence in this collection of the minute books of a Dublin club of the Apprentice Boys of Derry from 1813 to 1911. The united diocese of Down, Dromore and Connor established a library in Belfast in 1854, and by 1899 it was of sufficent significance to have a printed catalogue which included descriptions of that part of the manuscripts of William Reeves (bishop of Down and Connor, 1886–92) purchased by the dioceses after the bishop's death.[33] These manuscripts, which are mostly copies in whole or in part by Reeves, relate largely to ecclesiastical affairs in counties Antrim and Down (papal taxations, visitations, details of clergy, illustrations of churches) and complement the other parts of Reeves's archive in the Royal Irish Academy, Trinity College, Dublin, and the Armagh Public Library: they are now in the Public Record Office, Belfast. R.G.S. King, dean of Derry, produced a short title catalogue of the Derry Cathedral Library in 1939 which includes brief accounts of two useful local collections. The Munn collection consists of thirty-two volumes of transcripts of records in British and Irish repositories relating to the city and county of Derry, while the papers of the noted record agent, Tenison Groves, include material about the city of Derry which was gleaned, in part, from sources in the Public Record Office of Ireland before the fire of 1922.[34]

30 For an overview of diocesan libraries see Maura Tallon, *Church of Ireland diocesan libraries* (Dublin, 1959) & Mary Casteleyn, *A history of libraries in Ireland* (Aldershot, 1984), pp 71–83. **31** N.J.D. White (ed.), *Catalogue of the manuscripts remaining in Marsh's Library, Dublin* (Dublin, N.D.). A revised edition of this catalogue is available on the Marsh's Library website – www.kst.dit.ie/marsh **32** James Dean, *Catalogue of manuscripts in the Public Library of Armagh* (Dundalk, 1928). Catalogue entries for the Armagh manuscripts are also available on the Library' website – www.armaghrobinsonlibrary.org **33** J.R. Garstin, 'Descriptive catalogue of the Bishop Reeves' collection of manuscripts' in *Down and Connor and Dromore Library: catalogue of books in the diocesan collections …* (Belfast, 1899). **34** R.G.S. King, *St Columb's cathedral, Londonderry: Chapter house library: short title catalogue* (Londonderry, 1939).

A catalogue of the Cashel Diocesan Library was published in 1973,[35] and to it was appended brief descriptions of the Library's small manuscript collection. However, apart from the early catalogues of the Library, which was amassed by Theophilus Bolton (archbishop of Cashel, 1730–44) and a catalogue of the library of William King (archbishop of Dublin, 1703–29) which formed the core of Bolton's collection, there is little of direct Church of Ireland interest among the manuscripts. There is no catalogue of the Ross Cathedral Library in Rosscarbery, County Cork and in any case the collection has been largely dispersed. However, the brief description of it in Maura Tallon's study of Church of Ireland diocesan libraries, although largely obsolete, is in one respect still useful for she provides a description of the only manuscript in the collection: the late eighteenth-century survey by Thomas Sherrard of the estates in County Cork of Sir John Freke, which shows portions of many of the parishes in the dioceses of Cork and Ross.

Somewhat different in character to these library catalogues is Hector Love's catalogue of the records of the archbishop of Armagh[36] which lists briefly, in index form, the contents of the diocesan registry in Vicars' Hill, Armagh. The catalogue is, given its format, inevitably of limited use and has been superseded by Anthony Malcomson's comprehensive catalogue compiled in the late 1970s after the collection was deposited in the Public Record Office of Northern Ireland. However, its real value lies in the simple fact of its being widely available in published form whereas Dr Malcomson's work remains only as a reference tool in the Public Record Office. No other diocese has published a catalogue of its archives but there are a number of printed lists and catalogues of some of the testamentary and matrimonial collections which were in the diocesan registries. The index to the Dublin grant books (which included wills, administrations and marriage licences) from the early seventeenth century to 1858 appeared in 1895[37] and was quickly followed by Sir Arthur Vicars's index to the prerogative wills of Ireland, 1536–1810,[38] H.F. Berry's edition of the register of wills and inventories of the diocese of Dublin for the years 1457–83[39] and indexes to the marriage licence bonds of Cork, Cloyne and Ross for the seventeenth and eighteenth centuries.[40] Between 1909 and 1920 five volumes of indexes to Irish wills were published by Phillimore[41] and in 1930 Fr Wallace Clare's *Guide to copies and abstracts of Irish wills* appeared.[42] More recently indexes to

35 *Catalogue of the Cashel diocesan library* (Boston, 1973).   36 H.W. Love, *Records of the archbishops of Armagh being an indexed catalogue of the manuscripts, documents and books in the archiepiscopal registry of Armagh* (Dundalk, 1965).   37 Published as appendices to the 26th & 30th *Report of the deputy keeper of the public records … Ireland* (Dublin, 1895 & 1899).   38 Arthur Vicars, *Index to the prerogative wills of Ireland, 1536–1810* (Dublin, 1897).   39 H.F. Berry, *Register of the wills and inventories of the diocese of Dublin …* (Dublin, 1898).   40 H.B. Gillman, *Index to the marriage licence bonds of the diocese of Cork and Ross … 1623–1750* (Cork, 1896–7) and G.H. Green, *Index to the marriage licence bonds of the diocese of Cloyne … 1630–1800* (Cork, 1899–1900).   41 W.P.W. Phillimore (ed.), *Indexes to Irish wills. i. Ossory, Leighlin, Ferns, Kildare* (London, 1909); ii. *Cork and Ross, Cloyne* (London, 1910); Gertrude Thrift (ed.), *Indexes to Irish wills. iii. Cashel and Emly, Waterford and Lismore, Killaloe and Kilfenora, Limerick, Ardfert and Aghadoe* (London, 1913); iv. *Dromore, Newry and Mourne* (London, 1918); v. *Derry and Raphoe* (London, 1920).   42 Wallace Clare, *A guide to copies and abstracts of Irish wills* (1930; reprint, Baltimore, 1989).

wills, administrations and marriage licence bonds have been published in the *Irish Ancestor*.[43]

However, if there are few catalogues of Irish ecclesiastical records and even fewer exclusively devoted to the archives of the Church of Ireland, there are a number of general source books which discuss Church of Ireland records. Among the best of these are *Irish church records*,[44] *Sources for early modern Irish history*[45], *Irish towns: a guide to sources*[46] and *Tracing the past*[47] which have valuable chapters on ecclesiastical records, while *Sources of Irish local history*,[48] despite being a little dated, is still useful. *Irish records*[49] and *Tracing your Irish ancestors*,[50] although written chiefly from a genealogical perspective, are also helpful, particularly the former which includes sketch maps of the parishes in each county. Similar maps are printed in *A new genealogical atlas of Ireland*.[51] *British sources for Irish history, 1485–1641*[52] contains some nuggets of Church of Ireland material in local repositories in Great Britain, such as a list of entries from the Court of Faculties muniment books in Lambeth Palace Library, London, which has information on clergy in Meath, Kildare, Down, Dublin and Wexford, and *Papers of British churchmen, 1780–1940*[53] has brief descriptions of the collections of Church of Ireland bishops and clergy in repositories in Great Britain and Ireland.

While published histories, catalogues and guides can provide an important introduction to local research, they are, in most instances, only part of the preparation for the real work which will require the use of original source material with all the challenges of access and interpretation that such endeavour involves. However, a useful bridge between printed and manuscript material is the not inconsiderable body of published editions, both complete text editions and detailed calendars of archives and manuscripts, which is available. Such works have a number of obvious advantages. First they are published and therefore available in research libraries, although in the case of older editions which may have been produced in limited numbers, they may not be as generally accessible as might be wished. Secondly, they are printed and therefore easier to read than the original documents, and, in the case of manuscripts which have been written in a language other than English, they may also provide a translation. Thirdly, they invariably include an introduction, usually by an expert in the field, which provides intellectual access to what otherwise may appear to be an obscure text, and an index which allows a more selective use of the source than would otherwise be possible.

43 These are listed in D.F. Begley (ed.), *Irish genealogy*, pp 167–70. **44** Raymond Refaussé, 'Records of the Church of Ireland' in J.G. Ryan (ed.), *Irish church records* (2nd ed., Dublin, 2001). **45** R.W. Dudley Edwards & Mary O'Dowd, *Sources for early modern Irish history, 1534–1641* (Cambridge, 1985). **46** Raymond Refaussé, 'Church records' in William & Anngret Simms (eds), *Irish towns: a guide to sources* (Dublin, 1988), pp 137–46. **47** William Nolan, *Tracing the past: sources for local studies in the Republic of Ireland* (Dublin, 1982). **48** T.P. O'Neill, *Sources for Irish local history* (Dublin, 1958). **49** J.G. Ryan, *Irish records: sources for family and local history* (Dublin, 1988). **50** John Grenham, *Tracing your Irish ancestors* (Dublin, 1992). **51** Brian Mitchell, *A new genealogical atlas of Ireland* (Baltimore, 1988). **52** B.C. O'Donovan & David Edwards, *British sources for Irish history, 1485–1641: a guide to manuscripts in local, regional and specialised repositories in England, Scotland and Wales* (Dublin, 1997). **53** *Papers of British churchmen, 1780–1940* (London, 1987).

The written legacy of the early Church is relatively well served by printed editions of texts of annals, lives of the saints and liturgical works, many of which are
closely associated with particular localities. Individual editions of the most famous of
the insular manuscripts, the Book of Kells,[54] Book of Durrow[55] and Book of
Armagh,[56] are readily available while other less famous but equally important liturgical texts, such as the Antiphonary of Bangor, County Down,[57] and the Martyrology
of Tallaght[58] have been published by the Henry Bradshaw Society or, like the
Kilcormac missal from County Offaly, printed as part of the transactions of the Royal
Irish Academy.[59] Charles Plummer's *Lives of the Irish saints*[60] is an invaluable introduction to Irish hagiography with the added bonus of texts in both Irish and English,
while Gearóid Mac Niochaill's booklet on medieval annals provides a valuable cri-
tique of the topic and a useful bibliography of manuscript and printed sources.[61]

Happily a good many of the, admittedly few, extant medieval Irish Church
archives have been printed. There are editions of all but one of the seven medieval
registers of the archbishops of Armagh,[62] of the two surviving Dublin diocesan registers[63] and the Black Book of Limerick.[64] The Red Book of Ossory,[65] Black and
White Books of Christ Church cathedral, Dublin, have been calendared,[66] and there
are editions of the Christ Church book of obits and martyology[67] and of the fourteenth-century account rolls.[68] For St Patrick's cathedral, Dublin, editions of the
Dignitas Decani[69] and the Dublin Troper[70] have been published, while Monck

---

54 There are a number of editions of the Book of Kells of which the 1990 facsimile edition with an
accompanying volume of commentary, edited by Peter Fox, is the most complete.   **55** A.A. Luce,
G.O. Simms, P. Meyer, L. Bieler, *Evangeliorum quattuor codex Durmacensis* (2 vols, Olten, Lausanne &
Freiburg, 1960).   **56** John Gwynn (ed.), *The book of Armagh* (Dublin, 1913).   **57** F.E. Warren (ed.),
The antiphonary of Bangor (2 vols, London, 1893 & 1895).   **58** R.I. Best & H.J. Lawlor (eds), *The mar-
tyrology of Tallaght* (London, 1931).   **59** H.J. Lawlor, 'The Kilcormac missal' in *Transactions of the Royal
Irish Academy,* xxxi, pt x (Dublin, 1900), pp 393–430.   **60** Charles Plummer, *Bethada Naem nErenn:
Lives of the Irish saints* (2 vols, Oxford, 1922).   **61** Gearoid MacNiocaill, *The medieval Irish annals* (Dublin,
1975).   **62** D.A. Chart (ed.), *The register of John Swayne ... 1418–1439* (Belfast, 1935); L.P. Murray,
'Archbishop Cromer's Register' in *Louth Arch. Soc. Jn.,* vi & vii (1926–30); W.G.H. Quigley & E.F.D.
Roberts (eds), *Registrum Johannis Mey ... 1443–1439* (Belfast, 1972); Brendan Smith (ed.), *The register of
Milo Sweetman ... 1361–1380* (Dublin, 1996); idem, *The register of Nicholas Fleming ... 1404–1416* (Dublin,
2003); M.A. Sughi, *The register of Octavian de Palatio ... 1478–1513* (2 vols, Dublin, 1999).   **63** J.T. Gilbert,
Crede mihi (Dublin, 1897); Charles McNeill (ed.), *Calendar of Archbishop Alen's register* (Dublin, 1950).
64 James McCafferty (ed.), *The black book of Limerick* (Dublin, 1907).   **65** H.J. Lawlor, 'A calendar of
the Liber Ruber of the diocese of Ossory' in *RIA Proc.,* xxvii, sect. C, no. 5 (1908), pp 159–208.   **66**
H.J. Lawlor, 'A calendar of the Liber Niger and Liber Albus of Christ Church, Dublin' in *RIA Proc.,*
xxvii, sect. C, no. 1 (1908), pp 1–93. Lawlor's calendar should be used in association with Aubrey
Gwynn, 'Some unpublished texts from the Black Book of Christ Church, Dublin' in *Analecta Hibernica,*
no. 16 (1946), pp 281–337.   **67** J.C. Crossthwaite (ed.), *The book of obits and martyrology of the cathedral
of the Holy Trinity, Dublin* (Dublin, 1844). A more recent edition of the book of obits is contained in
Raymond Refaussé & Colm Lennon (eds), *The registers of Christ Church cathedral, Dublin* (Dublin, 1998).
68 James Mills (ed.), *Account roll of the priory of Holy Trinity, Dublin, 1337–1346* (Dublin, 1891). A new
edition of Mills' work was published in 1996 with introductions by James Lydon & A.J. Fletcher.   **69**
N.B. White (ed.), *The 'Dignitas Decani' of St Patrick's cathedral, Dublin* (Dublin, 1957).   **70** *Le tropaire-
prosaire de Dublin* (Rouen, 1966).

Mason's history of the cathedral reproduces the texts a number of individual documents.[71] The records of other monastic houses, apart from Christ Church cathedral, are also printed. Substantial Dublin foundations such as St Mary's Abbey,[72] the Priory of All Hallows[73] and the Abbey of St Thomas[74] were obviously attractive to editors but registers of rural houses such as the priory at Tristernagh, near Kilbixy, County Westmeath,[75] were also printed, as were cartularies (monastic registers) from British houses with Irish associations like the Augustinian foundation of Llanthony[76] which had houses in Monmouthshire, Gloucestershire and County Meath. Shorter pieces, such as the fifteenth and sixteenth-century episcopal rentals of Clonfert and Kilmacduagh, have appeared from time to time in *Analecta Hibernica.*[77]

Church archives from the modern period have also been printed but, in proportion to the quantity of material available, the output has been much less than for the medieval period. The Parish Register Society of Dublin published, between 1906 and 1915, twelve volumes of registers of baptisms, marriages and burials,[78] and in recent years the Representative Church Body Library has revived this project.[79] Moreover the initiation of an RCB Library 'Texts and Calendars' series has provided a vehicle for the publication of important vestry records.[80] In the field of diocesan archives editions of records such as the late seventeenth-century court book of St Sepulchre's, which was a liberty within the jurisdiction of the archbishop of Dublin.[81] and Bishop Dive Downes's visitation of the dioceses of Cork and Ross

71 William Monck Mason, *The history and antiquities of the collegiate and cathedral church of St Patrick near Dublin* ... (Dublin, 1820).   **72** J.T. Gilbert (ed.), *Chartularies of St Mary's abbey, Dublin* (2 vols, Dublin, 1884).   **73** Richard Butler (ed.), *Registrum prioratus omnium sanctorum* (Dublin, 1845).   **74** J.T. Gilbert (ed.), *Register of the abbey of St Thomas, Dublin* (Dublin, 1889).   **75** M.V. Clarke, *Register of the priory of the Blessed Virgin Mary at Tristernagh* (Dublin, 1941).   **76** E. St J. Brooks (ed.), *The Irish cartularies of Llanthony prima & secundus* (Dublin, 1953).   **77** K.W. Nicholls, 'The episcopal rentals of Clonfert and Kilmacduagh' in *Analecta Hibernica*, no. 26 (1970), pp 103–143.   **78** James Mills (ed.), *The register of St John the Evangelist, Dublin, 1619–1699* (Dublin, 1906, rep. 2000), *The register of the liberties of cashel, 1654–1657* (Dublin, 1907), *The registers of St Peter and St Kevin, Dublin, 1663–1761* (Dublin, 1911); J.H. Bernard (ed.), *The registers of St Patrick, Dublin, 1677–1800* (Dublin, 1907); H.J. Lawlor (ed.), *The registers of Provost Winter (Trinity College, Dublin), 1650–1660* (Dublin, 1907); H.S. Guinness (ed.), *The register of the union of Monkstown (co. Dublin), 1669–1786* (Dublin, 1908); Herbert Wood (ed.), *The registers of St Catherine, Dublin, 1636–1715* (Dublin, 1980, rep. 2003); H.F. Berry (ed.), *The registers of St Michan, 1636–1700* (Dublin, 1909); R. Hayes (ed.), *The register of Derry cathedral ... 1642–1703* (Dublin, 1910); D.A. Chart (ed.), *Marriage entries from the registers of St Andrew, St Anne, St Audeon & St Bride, 1632–1800* (Dublin, 1913); A.E. Langman (ed.), *Marriage entries in the registers ... S. Marie, S. Luke, S. Catherine & S. Werburgh, 1627–1800* (Dublin, 1915).   **79** Raymond Refaussé (ed.), *Register of the parish of St Thomas, Dublin, 1750–1791* (Dublin, 1994); idem, *Register of the church of St Thomas, Lisnagarvey, co. Antrim, 1637–1646* (Dublin, 1996); Colin Thomas (ed.), *Register of the cathedral church of St Columb, Derry, 1703–1732* (Dublin, 1997); idem, *Register of the cathedral church of St Columb, Derry, 1732–1775* (Dublin, 1999); Susan Hood (ed.), *Register of the parish of Holy Trinity, Cork, 1643–1668* (Dublin, 1998); Suzanne Pegley (ed.), *Register of the parish of Leixlip, Co. Kildare, 1665–1778* (Dublin, 2001); Brigid Clesham (ed.), *Register of the parish of St Nicholas, Galway, 1792–1840* (Dublin, 2004).   **80** Raymond Gillespie (ed.), *The vestry records of the parish of St John the Evangelist, Dublin, 1595–1658* (Dublin, 2002); idem, *The vestry records of the parishes of St Catherine and St James, Dublin, 1657–1692* (Dublin, 2004).   **81** Herbert Wood (ed.), *Court book of the liberty of Saint Sepulchre ... 1586–1590* (Dublin, 1930).

in 1699[82] have been valuable for local studies; and Raymond Gillespie's work on the early-modern muniments of Christ Church cathedral, Dublin, has done much to revive interest in cathedral communities.[83] Many smaller documents have been printed in the journals of local history societies and in the publications of national and provincial learned bodies. For example, the early nineteenth-century visitation records of Charles Lindsay, bishop of Kildare, appeared in the Kildare Archaeological Society's journal,[84] while Archbishop Bulkley's visitation of Dublin in 1630 was printed in *Archivium Hibernicum,* the journal of the Catholic Record Society of Ireland[85]. R.J. Hayes's compendious listing of articles in Irish periodicals[86] is an invaluable guide to such material.

Those primary sources which might not, in the most obvious sense of the word, be construed as archives – gravestones and memorials, church plate, portraits and stained glass – are also to varying extents accessible through the medium of published lists and indexes. The Association for the Preservation of the Memorials of the Dead, Ireland published an annual journal from 1888 to 1937 which included, in a rather chaotic fashion, inscriptions from many Church of Ireland graveyards and, more recently, the Ulster Historical Foundation has sponsored a *Gravestone Inscriptions* series which has catalogued many Church of Ireland graveyards in counties Antrim and Down.[87] Much additional transcription has been done by, for example, Brian Cantwell in counties Wicklow and Wexford and Michael Egan in Dublin,[88] and many enthusiastic amateurs continue this good work throughout the country and publish their transcriptions in local history and genealogical journals. A number of catalogues of church plate have been published, notably Webster's illustrated catalogue of the plate of the dioceses of Cork, Cloyne and Ross which has been usefully augmented by the work of Bowen and O'Brien,[89] Seymour's list of the plate of Cashel and Emly,[90] and Tony Sweeny's illustrated catalogue of Irish Stuart silver[91] which includes references to many Church of Ireland pieces, while an impression of the Church's collection of portraits may be had from a list which was published in 1916.[92] A useful general introduction to Church of Ireland plate,

---

82 T.A. Lunham (ed.), 'Bishop Dive Downes' visitation of his diocese in 1699' in *Cork Hist. Soc. Jn.,* vols xiv & xv (1908–9).   **83** Raymond Gillespie (ed.), *The proctor's accounts of Peter Lewis, 1574–1575* (Dublin, 1996); idem (ed.), *The first chapter act book of Christ Church cathedral, Dublin, 1574–1700* (Dublin, 1997); idem, *Thomas Howell and his friends: serving Christ Church cathedral, Dublin, 1570–1700* (Dublin, 1997); idem, 'Borrowing books from Christ Church' in *Long Room,* no. 43 (1998).   **84** Raymond Refaussé, 'The visitation note book of Charles Lindsay, bishop of Kildare' in *Kildare Arch. Soc. Jn.,* xvii (1991).   **85** M.V. Ronan, 'Archbishop Bulkley's visitation of Dublin, 1630' in *Archivium Hibernicum,* viii (1941).   **86** R.J. Hayes (ed.), *Sources for the history of Irish Civilization: articles in Irish periodicals.*   **87** R.S.J. Clarke (ed.), *Gravestone inscriptions, county Down* (20 vols, Belfast, 1986–9); idem, *Gravestone inscriptions, county Antrim* (3 vols, Belfast, 1977–95); idem, *Gravestone inscriptions, Belfast* (4 vols, Belfast, 1982–91). **88** The work of Cantwell and Egan is available in typescript in the major Dublin repositories.   **89** C.A. Webster, *The church plate of the diocese of Cork, Cloyne and Ross* (Cork, 1909); J.R. Bowen & Conor O'Brien, *Cork silver and gold: four centuries of craftsmanship* (Cork, 2005).   **90** St J. D. Seymour, *Church plate and parish records, diocese of Cashel and Emly* (Clonmel, 1930).   **91** Tony Sweeny, *Irish Stuart silver: catalogue raisonné* (Dublin, 1995).   **92** *Lists of oil paintings, mezzotints … in the possession of the bishops, deans, chapters and Representative Body of the Church of Ireland* (Dublin, 1916).

portraits and topographical prints and drawings is the catalogue of an exhibition which was held in the National Gallery of Ireland to mark the centenary of the disestablishment of the Church of Ireland.[93] There are no specific catalogues of Church of Ireland stained glass windows, but the works of Nicola Gordon Bowe, Lesley Whiteside and Michael Wynne contain much useful information on windows in Church of Ireland churches and cathedrals.[94]

PHYSICAL ACCESS: VISITING THE LIBRARIES AND ARCHIVES

When the histories have been scanned, the catalogues consulted, and the printed editions and their introductions ruthlessly pillaged, the time will be ripe for researchers to visit the repositories and other locations in which the archives and the manuscripts of the Church of Ireland are to be found. Such visits will allow researchers to follow up the leads which they have obtained from the introductory printed material but, more importantly, will introduce them to the great majority of Church of Ireland records which have not been edited for publication and which do not appear in printed catalogues.

Church of Ireland archives and manuscripts are to be found in two custodies – repositories, usually archives and libraries, both publicly and privately funded, and 'local custody', that is, with the clergy, church officers, parishes, dioceses, cathedrals and organizations that created the records. These two custodies present different challenges to the researcher and within both categories there will be variants of practice which may in turn delight and exasperate.

The collections in publicly funded repositories, in theory at least, are the most accessible, and those in the National Archives, National Library, Public Record Office of Northern Ireland, Trinity College, Dublin, and the Royal Irish Academy, in particular, cannot be ignored by any serious local historian who is interested in Church of Ireland archives and manuscripts. Although all these repositories depend upon government funding for their existence, their attitude to members of the public varies and the eager reader is not always given the impression of a right of public access to the collections. Formalities vary but may include the need to make an appointment, an interview and the issue of a reader's ticket for which a letter of introduction and a photograph may be necessary and for which a fee may be charged. Having been granted admission, readers will have to master the repository's finding aids which are the essential means of local intellectual access to the great mass of archives and manuscripts which have not been described in printed catalogues. This tends to be somewhat more daunting in the large public repositories since their collections are very various and the Church of Ireland dimension

93 *Church disestablishment 1870–1970: a centenary exhibition* (Dublin, 1970). 94 See James White & Michael Wynne, *Irish stained glass* (Dublin, 1963); Nicola Gordon Bowe, David Caron & Michael Wynne, *Gazetteer of Irish stained glass* (Dublin, 1988); Lesley Whiteside, *The stained glass of Christ Church cathedral, Dublin* (Dublin, 1999) & *The stained glass of St Patrick's cathedral, Dublin* (Dublin, n.d.).

within them is rarely a priority for the curatorial staff. In most institutions there will still be a card catalogue, either a single integrated catalogue or one which is divided thematically (places, persons, subjects etc.), which will provide initial access and references to summary typescript catalogues or detailed handlists of particular collections. These will allow researchers to establish more clearly the potential value of the material for their research. Increasingly, however, information about collections is available in computerized forms, either as individual lists or in searchable databases, some of which may be consulted via or even down-loaded from the internet. At a minimum, most institutions will have a website which will give introductory information about the repository and its collections: all researchers ought to consult such websites before contacting a repository.[95] For diligent researchers, who are prepared to spend time with each repository's finding aids, in whatever form they appear, there are great riches to be uncovered.

The National Archives, as the principal archival repository of the Irish State, remains a useful source for Church of Ireland material as, despite the enormous losses in 1922, much relevant material has been subsequently accessioned and invaluable copy and extract material has been obtained, which make good some of the losses. The original records of a number of parishes, the tithe applotment books for parishes in the Republic of Ireland, the surviving records of the Ecclesiastical Commissioners and the Irish Church Temporalities Commissioners, and the indexes to matrimonial and testamentary records are complemented by, for example, the growing collection of copy wills, a body of miscellaneous extracts and certified copies from parish registers, and copies of various diocesan and cathedral records. However, perhaps the single most significant Church of Ireland collection in the National Archives is the archive of the central administration of the Protestant Orphan Society,[96] which complements the records of the various county orphan societies.

In the National Library, the Department of Manuscripts has the most comprehensive collection of Irish family papers, and inevitably these include many little-known collections which illuminate local life from a Church of Ireland perspective. The papers of Robert Howard, successively bishop of Killala and Elphin in the first half of the eighteenth century,[97] are, as the work of Toby Barnard has revealed, an invaluable source for studying learning and literacy in the west of Ireland,[98] while the collections of Church of Ireland families such as Smyth of Barbavilla, County Westmeath,[99] or converts to anglicanism like French of Monivea, County Galway,[1] can document in extraordinary detail the lives of many who lived in the localities in which such families held sway.

For those whose research is based on places or people in Northern Ireland, or to a lesser extent in the other three counties of the historic province of Ulster, a visit to

95 Website addresses for Irish repositories are given in Helfery & Refaussé, *Directory of Irish archives.* **96** National Archives acc. no. 1045. **97** NLI, PC 227. **98** Toby Barnard, 'Learning, the learned and literacy in Ireland, *c.* 1660–1760' in Toby Barnard, Daibhí Ó Croinín & Katherine Simms (eds), *A miracle of learning ...: essays in honour of William O'Sullivan* (Aldershot, 1998), pp 209–35. **99** NLI MS, unlisted collection. **1** See D.A. Cronin, *A Galway gentleman in the age of improvement: Robert French of* the Public Record Office in Belfast is essential. In archival terms PRONI is, in effect, the Church of Ireland repository for Northern Ireland (rather in the same way in which each diocese of the Church of England usually nominates one of the county record offices as the diocesan record centre) and holds considerable collections of parish and diocesan records as well as the tithe applotment books for parishes in Northern Ireland. Most Church of Ireland parish registers, in copy or original form, are available there, and a number of parishes have deposited other categories of records – vestry minute books, accounts, preachers' books etc. Records from the dioceses of Armagh, Clogher, Derry, Down and Dromore, and Connor have been transferred to Belfast. In addition, like the Representative Church Body Library in Dublin, PRONI holds collections of papers of significant church figures such as Lord John George Beresford (archbishop of Armagh, 1822–62)[2] and the antiquarian cleric, W.A. Reynell, who copied much valuable material from the Board of First Fruits Office,[3] as well as records of local organizations like the Protestant Orphan Society[4] or the Belfast Church Extension Society which chart the development of the Church of Ireland in the developing suburbs of the city in the late nineteenth and early twentieth century.[5] Also included in the collections are papers of the great anglican titled families like the Abercorns, Downshires and Dunleaths who contributed much to the Church especially in rural Ulster;[6] and a bewildering array of civil archives, photographs and miscellaneous papers which can illuminate innumerable aspects of the life of the Church of Ireland in many localities.

The same is true of the Manuscripts Room in the Library of Trinity College, Dublin, whose printed catalogues cover only a fraction of the Church of Ireland material which is available. Most importantly, there is no published guide to the large collection of College records which bear on the Church of Ireland in many ways. The College, as we have seen, was founded in the late sixteenth century, essentially as a Church of Ireland seminary, and until this century the vast majority of its students were Church of Ireland. Moreover, until 1873 its fellows had to be Church of Ireland clergy although there were dispensations from this obligation. Until 1980 Church of Ireland clergy were trained in the College's divinity school, and until 1973 the services in the College chapel were exclusively Church of Ireland. Therefore, the documentation, which the administration of the College produced, inevitably, is an important source for the Church of Ireland, not only in Dublin and not only in the area of university education, but throughout Ireland, for clergy who trained in Trinity served in parishes in every part of the country and brought their own particular flavour to local life. Furthermore the College owned extensive landed estates in Ulster and Munster and the associated advowsons of a number of parishes. These positions were largely reserved for fellows of the College who wished to return to parish life, and so a significant number of parishes enjoyed clergy of unusual intellectual eminence and occasional eccentricity. The historian, Thomas Leland, resigned his fellowship in 1781 to become rector of Newtownstewart in the wilds

Monivea, 1716–79 (Dublin, 1995). **2** PRONI D664 & D3279. **3** PRONI DIO/1. **4** PRONI MIC/520. **5** PRONI DIO/1. **6** PRONI D/623, D/607 & 671, D/4179,.

of County Tyrone, while in 1822 the astronomer and mathematician, Thomas Romney Robinson, later to become president of the Royal Irish Academy, resigned to become rector of Enniskillen.[7] Much information on the background of the local clergy and the careers of the fellows may be obtained from the College muniments.

As in the case of the muniments, many of the manuscript collections are not detailed in published catalogues. Abbott's *Catalogue* appeared in 1900, and there has been no general catalogue published since then, so researchers must depend on in-house lists and indexes for information on subsequent accessions. The Trinity collection includes episcopal correspondence such as that of the nineteenth-century bishop of Limerick, John Jebb,[8] or William Bennet,[9] who became bishop of Cork in 1790; diaries like those of the Revd Daniel Beaufort detailing his travels in Ireland in the early nineteenth century;[10] letters of local clergy such as the Revd Charles Claudius Beresford who was rector of Bailieborough in County Cavan during the Great Famine.[11] In addition there are copies of, now lost, ecclesiastical records such as those made by William Reeves, bishop of Down and Connor, largely from sources in the Public Record Office of Ireland[12] and those of the Cork antiquary, Richard Caulfield (1823–87), from the Cork diocesan archives.[13] Furthermore the records of organizations with close associations with the Church of Ireland such as the Irish Society,[14] the Island and Coast Society[15] and the Hibernian Marine Society[16] contain valuable information on those who were involved in missionary and educational work on the geographical peripheries of Ireland.

In the Royal Irish Academy the papers of William Reeves, bishop of Down and Connor, the Revd James Graves (1815–86), the renowned Irish antiquarian, and H.R. Dawson (dean of St Patrick's cathedral, Dublin, 1828–40) who corresponded on historical and antiquarian subjects with among others, Richard Butler, vicar of Trim, James Saurin, archdeacon of Dromore, and George Dwyer, rector of Ardrahan, County Galway,[17] are all of potential local interest. So too are stray Church of Ireland archives such as visitations of the diocese of Ossory in 1845 and 1848,[18] and copies of now lost records such as appear in James Ferguson's precises of documents (leases, grants, letters) relating to parishes in the dioceses of Dublin and Glendalough from the fourteenth to the nineteenth century,[19] and copies of records (rentals, tithe records, visitations) of the dioceses of Down and Connor in the seventeenth and eighteenth centuries.[20] Perhaps the richest source for local studies among the Academy's manuscript collections and one which includes much about the Church of Ireland is the Ordnance Survey memoirs and related papers. These contain detailed accounts of many of the parishes of Ireland in the mid-nineteenth century and inevitably include much valuable information about buildings

7 Details of clerical fellows who resigned to take up parochial appointments may be had from J.R. Bartlett (ed.), *Trinity College, Dublin, record volume 1991* (Dublin, 1992). 8 TCD MS 2321a, 6396–7. 9 TCD MS 4326. 10 TCD MS 4024, 4026–31, 4033, 4037, 5118. 11 TCD MS 2288 & 2288a. 12 TCD MS 2904–11, 3760. 13 TCD MS 2010–15. 14 TCD MS 7644–62. 15 TCD MS 7664–8. 16 TCD MS 5134–5202d. 17 RIA MS 4.B.36. 18 RIA MS 24.Q.32–3. 19 RIA MS 12.D.25. 20 RIA MS 24.K.25.

which had been or continued to be used as Church of Ireland churches and cathedrals. The forty published volumes of memoirs[21] cover the counties of Antrim, Armagh, Donegal, Down, Fermanagh, Londonderry and Tyrone with some additional material for counties Cavan, Leitrim, Louth, Monaghan and Sligo. The complementary thirty-five volumes of letters, of which volumes for only five counties have been published,[22] contain 'information relative to the antiquities' of virtually every parish in the country.

The Representative Church Body Library in Dublin is the Church of Ireland's repository for its archives and manuscripts, and all researchers are welcome to use its facilities: basic information on how to get there and what to expect is available on the Church of Ireland website.[23] Essentially the Library holds those non-current records of the Church of Ireland in the Republic of Ireland which the parishes, dioceses, cathedrals and central administration have chosen to transfer to it, together with a small quantity of similar records from Northern Ireland. There is as yet no requirement to transfer non-current records to the Library and the extent to which transfers have occurred varies throughout the country. There is, therefore, nothing inevitable about the Library's archival holdings and some materials which researchers might reasonably expect to have been transferred may still be in 'local custody'. The Library's holdings are further defined by legislation: older parish registers[24] are public records in Northern Ireland and national archives in the Republic and may not be moved from one political jurisdiction to the other. To avoid splitting collections, some parishes have elected to deposit all their non-current records to the Public Record Office in Belfast rather than divide their collections between PRONI and the RCB Library.

At present the Library holds records from over 900 parishes, seventeen dioceses, and twenty cathedrals, mostly in the Republic of Ireland; the minutes, reports and related documentation of the General Synod, Representative Church Body, and their statutory committees, since disestablishment; and the records of a variety of fixed term committees and commissions which have been set up to examine particular aspects of the Church's life. Access to most of this material is straightforward. The *Constitution of the Church of Ireland* explicitly recognizes a right of public access to all parish registers of baptisms, marriages and burials and so there are no restrictions on making these records available. Otherwise, the Library operates in accordance with normal archival procedures: there is a thirty-year rule (that is, records which are less than thirty years old are not usually made available to researchers) and material which is deemed to be of a sensitive nature may be closed for longer periods. In the particular case of the manuscript records of the General Synod, the

21 Angélique Day & Patrick McWilliams (eds), *Ordnance survey memoirs of Ireland* (40 vols, Belfast, 1990–8). **22** Micheal Herity (ed.), *Ordnance survey letters, Donegal* (Dublin, 2000); idem, *Ordnance survey letters, Meath* (Dublin, 2001); idem, *Ordnance survey letters, Dublin* (Dublin, 2001); idem, *Ordnance survey letters, Down* (Dublin, 2001); idem, *Ordnance survey letters, Kildare* (Dublin, 2002); idem, *Ordnance survey letters, Kilkenny* (Dublin, 2003). **23** www.ireland.anglican.org/ **24** Registers of baptisms & burials up to and including the year 1870 and registers of marriages up to and including 31 March 1845.

12 Architectural drawing of Ballycahane church, County Limerick

House of Bishops and Representative Church Body a forty-year rule is in operation. However, the vast majority of Church of Ireland archives are available for
consultation without restriction.

One class of record in the Library which sits a little apart from the official
archives of the Church is the large body of architectural drawings which may be a
stray remnant of the archive of the Ecclesiastical Commissioners. The component
parts of this collection are a six-volume survey of churches in the ecclesiastical
province of Cashel by James Pain, dating probably from the second quarter of the
nineteenth century;[25] four mid-nineteenth century volumes of drawings of churches
largely, but not exclusively, in the province of Tuam, and mostly by Joseph
Welland;[26] and twenty-seven portfolios of drawings of churches from all parts of
Ireland, by various architects, dating from the 1830s to the 1860s with more recent
accessions.[27] Both Pain and Welland were distinguished architects, having worked
for the Board of First Fruits and the Ecclesiastical Commissioners, as were figures
such as William Atkins, Frederick Darley, and the partnership of Lanyon and Lynn,
whose work is also represented in the collections.

25 RCBL MS 138. **26** RCBL MS 139. **27** RCBL, records of the Representative Church Body.

In addition to the official archives of the Church of Ireland the Library holds some 750 collections of miscellaneous manuscripts consisting for the most part of papers of clergy and laity and records of voluntary organizations closely related to the Church of Ireland.

In recent years the Library has become a focus for the papers of bishops, clergy and laity. Episcopal collections, such as the correspondence of Euseby Cleaver who was bishop of Ferns at the time of the 1798 rebellion[28] and Lord John Beresford who was archbishop of Armagh at the height of the tithe war in the 1830s,[29] can provide valuable local insights into national events. The diaries of the Revd Stephen Gwynn are a useful window into north Antrim life in the second half of the nineteenth century;[30] the daily weather notes of Henry Cotton, archdeacon of Cashel, for the 1820s and 1830s provide a period insight into a perennial topic of Irish conversation;[31] and the papers of Hugh Maude, a prominent County Dublin layman, reveal much about the Church of Ireland's response to constitutional, liturgical and administrative change in the 1940s and 1950s.[32] The research papers of clergy who had used local and national collections in the late nineteenth and early twentieth centuries have, since the destruction of 1922, assumed an enhanced significance, and there are useful examples of such collections in the Library apart from the papers of Leslie and his colleagues who worked on clerical successions. The notes of the Revd James Graves relating to the medieval diocese of Ossory, which were taken from the Irish memoranda and plea rolls,[33] the Revd St John Seymour's notes on the Commonwealth records[34] and the Revd W.H. Rennison's unpublished research into the history of the diocese of Waterford[35] are examples of this genre.

Equally rich as sources for the Church of Ireland in the localities are the records of a wide range of organizations and societies, mostly with their origins in the nineteenth century, which touched the faithful and those who were distressed in body, mind or estate. The records of the nineteenth- and twentieth-century clerical societies provide an entrée into the social, spiritual and educational world of local rectors, while organizations such as the Nenagh Young Men's Christian and Literary Association, founded in 1861 for the moral, educational and social advancement of the young men of the town,[36] or the City of Dublin Conservative Working Men's Club,[37] are interesting sources for the history of local recreation. The poor and disadvantaged are catalogued in the records of bodies such as the Protestant Orphan Society which was organized on a county basis[38] or the Association for the Relief of Distressed Protestants,[39] while the rescue of 'fallen women' is chronicled in the records of the Prison Gate Mission[40] and the Magdalen Asylum, Dublin.[41] The Church, too, was closely involved in the education of children and the training of

28 RCBL MS 328. **29** RCBL MS 183. **30** RCBL MS 440. **31** RCBL MS 117. **32** RCBL MS 262. **33** RCBL MS 11 & 581. **34** RCBL MS 21. **35** RCBL MS 40. **36** RCBL MS 550. **37** RCBL MS 486. **38** The records of the Protestant orphan societies for counties Carlow (MS 340), Cork (MS 519), Kerry (MS 527), Meath (MS 286), Monaghan (MS 692), Offaly (MS 501), Queen's (MS 723) & Sligo (MS 416) have been deposited in the RCB Library. **39** RCBL MS 485. **40** RCBL MS 263. **41** RCBL MS 551.

13 A page from Douglas Hyde's translation into Irish of
St Patrick's Breastplate

teachers. The records of bodies such as the Incorporated Society for Promoting Protestant Schools in Ireland, which had a presence in virtually every county in Ireland,[42] and the Church Education Society[43] reveal this in a national context while the administrative records of schools like the Irish Clergy Daughters' School, Dublin,[44] Bishop Foy's School, Waterford[45] and Bishop Hodson's Grammar School, Elphin,[46] provide evidence of such activity in the localities. The promotion of the Irish language in the Church of Ireland is reflected in the records of Comhluadar Gaodhalach na Fianaise (Irish Guild of Witness) and, more especially, Cumann Gaelachna hEaglaise (Irish Guild of the Church) and in the pages of its journal *An tEaglaiseach Gaelach (The Gaelic Churchman)* which was published from 1919 to 1927. The guild traces its origins to a request, in the early 1900s, from Sean O'Casey and Ernest Blythe that services in Irish might be held in St Kevin's church, Dublin, although it was not officially formed until 1914. In addition to promoting the use of Irish, it sought also to collect Irish sources suitable for hymns and devotional literature, and to encourage the use of Irish art and music.[47]

The archives of the Church and the records of organizations and individuals for the more recent past are complemented by the oral recollections and reminiscences of clergy and laity. The development of this oral archive is in its infancy, and most of the initial tranche of recordings will be closed to readers during the lifetime of the interviewees. However, the determination of the Church of Ireland to record the experiences not only of the leaders of the Church but also of the men and women in the pews suggests that, in time, this may be an invaluable supplement to the official record. Since the experiences of the majority of Church people are confined to a small number of localities, this promises to be a significant source for local studies. It also emphasizes the importance, for those whose research in centred on the recent past, of seeking out the experiences of older members of the community.

Like the oral history project, the photographic archive is a relatively recent innovation and still very much 'work in progress'. The majority of photographs which have been collected and commissioned are of church buildings, but there is a growing body of visual information on clergy, laity, events and artifacts, including church plate, stained glass windows and portraits.

Conditions of access to the manuscripts collection are similar to those which relate to Church of Ireland archives. A thirty-year rule is in operation, and some collections or parts of collections are closed for longer periods. There is no direct reader access, for reasons of sensitivity and security, to the oral archive, the church plate database and the database of portraits, but the Library staff will evaluate the validity of requests for information from these sources and, where appropriate, respond positively.

42 TCD MSS 5225–5859 & RCBL MS 151. **43** RCBL MS 154. **44** RCBL MS 357. **45** RCBL MS 523. **46** RCBL MS 354. **47** RCBL MSS 89 & 131; see also Leaslaoi Ó Briain, 'What! Have a service in Erse in St Patrick's? – Cuman Galeach na hEaglaise – 90 years young' in *Search*, vol. 27, no. 1, spring, 2004, pp 5–11.

Access to some of the other Church of Ireland repositories is less certain, although there is invariably a willingness to be accommodating. The two 'public libraries', Archbishop Marsh's Library in Dublin and Archbishop Robinson's Library in Armagh, are the most accessible, with regular staff and public opening hours.[48] Admittance to the collections in the diocesan libraries is dependent to a large extent on the availability of local custodians. It would, therefore, be prudent for researchers to write in advance, establishing their *bona fides* and stating clearly the material which they wish to see, and to follow up their letter with a telephone call to ensure that all is well before they travel.

In terms of access to Church of Ireland records, the greatest difficulties occur with material which is in 'local custody'. A significant quantity of parish records remains in local churches, rectories and parish offices, and access to them is through the medium of the local clergy whose addresses (increasingly both postal and e-mail), telephone numbers, and sometimes parish websites are usually the points of contact. The clergy are required by the *Constitution of the Church of Ireland* to 'at all reasonable times, on demand, allow search in such registers [of baptisms, marriages and burials]' and whilst there is a general willingness to accommodate researchers in the spirit of this obligation, nevertheless there are frequently practical problems in fulfilling it. Most obviously, problems arise because most Church of Ireland clergy work alone: few have curates and even fewer are part of a team ministry in which administrative responsibility can be shared among members of a group of clergy and laity. Some urban parishes will have an office in which researchers can consult parish records in a comfortable environment where they are supervised by parish officers, but this is the exception to the rule. In most instances 'local access' means that the local clergy must produce the records and personally supervise the search in a church vestry which will usually be a cold and unattractive location, or in the rectory, which is the clergy residence and in which researchers may, in effect, be intruding on family life. In consequence a lone cleric may, at times, be unable to accommodate researchers with the expedition that they consider to be appropriate. Researchers invariably believe that their work is a priority, and whilst it ought to be so for them it cannot always be so for clergy, who may have to conduct marriages, visit the sick and dying and bury the dead, among a host of other parochial duties, as well as considering the needs of their families.

Despite these potential difficulties it is important to stress that there is, in most instances, a ready willingness among local clergy to help, but researchers will greatly help themselves and increase the likelihood of ready access to the collections in which they are interested by taking some basic preparatory steps. They need first to establish not only that the records survive for a particular locality but that they are extant for the appropriate period, and then they must discover who has custody of these records. Inventories of most parish records are held in the Representative Church Body Library, and it is usually possible to advise researchers, with a reasonable degree of accuracy, if the records which they are seeking are extant. The

48 www.marshlibrary.ie & www.armaghrobinsonlibrary.org

contact details of the clergy and the churches for which they are responsible are published annually in the *Church of Ireland Directory*, which is available in printed form in most reference libraries or on the Church of Ireland website.[49] However, the *Directory* has three limitations. First, it concentrates on churches which are still open for worship, and some local research will require access to the records of closed churches and their parishes; secondly, there are frequent changes to the clerical directory in the course of a year and, as the *Directory* is an annual publication, parts of it can be out of date; and thirdly, there will from time to time be vacant parishes (that is, parishes without a resident priest or deacon) and so the *Directory* will not supply a contact name, address or telephone number. For those with access to the internet, the clerical directory on the Church of Ireland website is periodically updated during the year: otherwise, the easiest way of dealing with these deficiencies is to contact the Representative Church Body Library where the staff can supply information on redundant churches and details of local contacts.

Once a researcher has established that appropriate records survive and has determined who has custody of them, the following procedure is recommended. Write to the local custodian, setting out, as clearly as the introductory sources have permitted, which records are required, and enclose a letter of introduction from a College supervisor or clergyperson (protestant or catholic); follow up the letter after a short time with a telephone call to make an appointment to see the records; and immediately before travelling telephone again to ensure that the arrangement still obtains. If such arrangements do not produce access to local records, researchers should contact the Representative Church Body Library where the staff may be able to set up an appointment locally or arrange to have the records transferred temporarily to the Library for research purposes. Clergy are entitled to charge a fee for supervising searches and, whilst many do not ask for payment, researchers should be financially prepared.

49 www.ireland.anglican.org.

CHAPTER 3

The interpretation of Church of Ireland archives and manuscripts

Although the major challenge for those using Church of Ireland archives and man-uscripts may appear to be to identify, locate and gain access to them, yet these chal-lenges having been met, problems of interpretation may remain. In other words, it is one thing to find oneself eventually seated before the much sought-after materi-als, but it is a step further to make sense of their contents and to place them in an appropriate context, for there are both strengths and weaknesses about Church of Ireland records of which researchers need to be aware.

The most obvious strengths of Church of Ireland records are their chronolog-ical span and geographical scope. It is worth reiterating that the Church is the old-est extant institution in Ireland: older than the State, older than the municipalities, older than the schools and universities, older in short than all those Irish institutions which are constantly trumpeting their longevity in a seemingly endless round of anniversary celebrations. There may still be debate about when and in what cir-cumstances Christianity was brought to this country and there may still be differ-ences of opinion about the lines of succession from the early Church following the fracturing of Christianity in the west in the sixteenth century. Nonetheless what is beyond dispute is the venerability of the shared heritage of the Celtic and medieval Church in Ireland and the astonishing talent for survival which the Church of Ireland has exhibited since the Reformation. The monastic Church in Ireland; the dioce-ses, cathedrals and parishes, largely created by the Normans; the established Church which emerged from the Reformation; and the disestablished Church of Ireland which succeeded it in the late nineteenth century are the principal phases of a con-tinuum of Christian worship, the *written* legacy of which is or has been largely the responsibility of the Church of Ireland. The survival of manuscript material for some parts of Ireland over such an extended period offers remarkable scope for the per-ceptive and persistent local historian.

Inevitably, of course, the places, families and institutions which can be studied over a protracted period are limited, but what is, within the physical confines of the island of Ireland, almost all-encompassing are the locations in which the Church of Ireland, for good or ill, has had a presence or an effect. The establishment of the parish system and its development to meet the constantly changing needs of rural and urban life introduced the Church to old and new communities throughout the country. During the period of the established Church, in particular, the Church of Ireland as both a religious and civil power, touched the lives of most classes of Irish men and women. The nobility and gentry who occupied grand houses in town and country, worshipped in the great cathedrals, were leading lights in the parish churches, and exercised patronage in ecclesiastical livings. The agricultural classes were tenants of bishops, cathedral chapters and parishes and supported the Church, willingly or unwillingly, with their tithes. The teeming hordes in the cities and towns availed in life of the religious and social services that the Church had to offer, and in death filled the graveyards of the city and town churches.

However, wide though the chronological and geographical scope of Church of Ireland records can be, their usefulness is inevitably circumscribed by two key considerations: first the Church of Ireland was always a minority Church, and secondly, many of its records no longer survive. Even at the height of its powers the Church of Ireland never commanded the loyalty, nominal or otherwise, much less the affection, of the majority of the people of Ireland. Despite penal legislation and the clearly perceived social and economic advantages of membership, the Church 'as by law established' had to compete with the Roman Catholic Church and the dissenting traditions for the support of the people. Many families, therefore, have no Church of Ireland tradition while for others the links with the established Church were so nominal as to be of only passing significance. An elder son may have conformed to retain his family's ownership of land only to revert to the 'one true Church' when it was safe to do so, while 'notorious Methodists', as they were sometimes described in clergy visiting books, may have availed of the Church of Ireland only for the Christian rites of passage but did not allow such necessities to influence unduly their Wesleyan life style. More generally, tenants may have held land from, or may have been employed by Church of Ireland proprietors without any more than a perfunctory nod in the direction of anglicanism. Inevitably, therefore, the records of the Church of Ireland will not tell the full story of Irish communities and, furthermore, the story which they can tell has been inhibited by the loss of so many records. Late medieval and early-modern Irish society was less developed, less prosperous, less sophisticated and less stable than in England or continental Europe. It produced, relatively, fewer archives and manuscripts and did not develop or retain sufficient centres of learning which could have fostered an appreciation of the importance of such materials and which might have provided the environment in which the safe transmission of records from one generation to the next could have been ensured. There were no medieval universities in imitation of Bologna, Paris, Oxford or Cambridge, and the monasteries, once dissolved, were not replaced with any significant alternative centres of learning: the Catholic clergy were trained abroad while the Church of Ireland did not have a seminary until the foundation of Trinity College in 1592. The Viking invasions, the dissolution of the monasteries and the Reformation, the 1641 Rebellion, the Commonwealth, the Jacobite and Williamite wars, and the 1798 Rebellion produced a litany of violence and disorder which repeatedly violated the fragile Irish ecclesiastical archival infrastructure. Even when the archives of Church and State seemed secure, with the establishment of a Public Record Office in Dublin and the transfer to it of much of the surviving national documentation, the violence of civil war, in an act of supreme irony, reduced to ashes the written evidence of the nation which the protagonists in the conflict sought so passionately to define. The destruction of many of the records of parishes, dioceses, cathedrals and of the central government, of which the Church of Ireland was an integral part, dealt the Church an enormous blow, for despite the survival of copy material, the ingenious use of civil records, and the evidence of archaeology and architecture, parts of the history of many Church of Ireland communities cannot be adequately researched because the sources no longer exist.

But other parts of the history of the Church of Ireland cannot be researched for a different reason: because the Church will not allow it. There is a tendency, perhaps understandable in an age when freedom of information is increasingly taken to be a societal norm, to assume that there is an automatic right of access to Church of Ireland records for interested researchers: but this is not so. The Church of Ireland is a private organization and its archives, with the exception of parish registers, access to which is guaranteed under civil and ecclesiastical law, are owned totally and absolutely by the Church, which is not obliged to make them available for historical research. That the Church chooses to open most of its records to researchers may tend to obscure the basic fact that such availablity is a privilege and not a right, and there are occasions on which this privilege is not extended to researchers. This is particularly so in the context of more recent records which in the case of the Church of Ireland may involve almost any aspect of the Church's life since disestablishment. The Church of Ireland of the twentieth century, especially in the Republic of Ireland, was a small, closely knit community with a long memory, and this continues to be the case in the twenty-first century. All of this makes it, at times, particularly cautious about publicly discussing aspects of its affairs which it considers to be sensitive. Thus, for example, the records of the central administration are closed for forty years; there is often a reluctance on the part of local custodians to allow researchers to trawl through post-disestablishment parish financial and administrative records; while the records of many charitable bodies are closed for what may appear to readers to be unreasonably long periods but which, in the context of a small community which values the privacy of its members, seems entirely appropriate. Such limitations on research may irritate readers and there may be a temptation to seek to circumvent restrictions on collections by personal appeals to higher authorities within the Church. Such activity is invariably counterproductive for it will result in the researcher losing the goodwill of the archival community.

Yet despite destruction and restriction, a sufficient corpus of material is available to allow at least a partial historical reconstruction of much of the Church's history. However, the effective use of much of this material is inhibited because it is uncatalogued, and of that which has been processed, many collections would benefit from more detailed archival attention. This is particularly true of the larger diocesan and cathedral archives and some of the more significant collections of papers of modern churchmen which contain considerable quantities of individual documents that are very time-consuming to process. These need to be sorted,

arranged and listed before being made available to researchers, not only for administrative and security purposes, but also because the production of a detailed han-
dlist, as well as providing descriptions of the individual elements of the collection,
place those items in an overall context which itself can be informative for researchers.
Irish archival life has developed significantly in recent years but is still enormously
under-resourced, and it is difficult to be optimistic that in the short term the considerable cataloguing backlogs, both in the Church of Ireland repositories, and in
the publicly funded archives and libraries which hold significant Church of Ireland
material, can be substantially reduced. Ironically the upsurge in interest in local history and the demands of researchers for information, advice and access to records
are among the main reasons for the continued problems with cataloguing: more
researchers occupy more staff time and leave even less than before for cataloguing!
An inevitable consequence of these problems of cataloguing has been a lack of
printed guides to Church of Ireland collections in the various repositories. Such
publications, by their very nature, are distillations of generations of detailed handlists, but since much of that basic work for the Church of Ireland has yet to be
done, the publication of guides would be premature.

This lack of handlists and guides has the unfortunate consequence of making
researchers too dependent on the small archival community who professionally service Church of Ireland collections. These archivists and librarians are not teachers,
they may not necessarily have an historical background, they may not even be members of the Church of Ireland, and they certainly are not polymaths. Most will know
a certain amount about the collections in their care, but they will not have an ency-
clopaedic knowledge about all aspects of all collections, and there is an inevitabil-
ity that their advice will be coloured more by the state of their particular knowledge rather than by their possession of a comprehensive overview of Church of
Ireland sources. Furthermore, in the larger national institutions, there is a tendency
to move curatorial staff from department to department, and whilst this ensures a
greater degree of professional flexibility within an institution, it also militates against
archival staff remaining long enough in a post to build up a substantial body of
knowledge about the collections in their care. The lack of finding aids creates problems not only for students but also for teachers, a significant number of whom seem
to be poorly informed about the holdings of many Irish repositories and assume that
curatorial staff will direct their students. It cannot be sufficiently stressed that archivists
and librarians are not directors of studies and that students who assume that they
are will most likely be disappointed.

The interpretation of Church of Ireland records, in a more particular sense, may
require a range of linguistic and palaeographic skills which are now rarely taught.
One of the less obvious strengths of post-Reformation Church of Ireland records is
that they are almost invariably written in English, in contrast to Roman Catholic
records for which Latin continued to be the language of record until the reforms of
the Second Vatican Council. However, those who intend to work on the archives
of the medieval Church will require a knowledge of Latin and, in some instances,

of Norman French which was the administrative language of the Norman kings of England, for while many of the texts have been printed, not all have been translated. A competence in school Latin, aided by a good dictionary and Baxter and Johnston's *Medieval Latin word-list*[1] will usually suffice, but those with no Latin at all need to consider whether the time spent in word-for-word translation is justifiable when so much material is available in English. Yet even those records which are written in English may present some problems for those who are not familiar with earlier forms of writing, particularly in the sixteenth and seventeenth centuries. However, the understanding of handwriting is, in most instances, a matter of familiarity, and frequent exposure to manuscript texts, with the assistance, initially, of a palaeographic guide,[2] will satisfy the needs of most researchers. From the middle of the eighteenth century handwritten English, with the exception of the use of the long letter S (similar to a modern letter F), is sufficiently similar to modern usage so as to present no real problems for modern readers: however, archaic forms of writing continued to be used occasionally until late in the century. But if the forms of the letters are fairly obvious from the 1780s on, there remains the eternal problem of bad handwriting which can render obscure even the simplest communication. The Church of Ireland did not begin to use typewriters for its central records until the 1930s, while at local level, handwritten minutes were the norm until the 1960s, and handwriting continues to be the form in which parish registers are maintained.

Those who find difficulty with handwriting may be tempted to resort to seeking photocopies of documents which can be examined at greater leisure outside the repositories. However, the provision of photocopies, and the whole area of reprography generally, can pose problems for the uninitiated student. Most repositories will no longer photocopy manuscript material, on conservation grounds, but they may offer, as alternatives, the provision of a photograph, a microfilm printout or a digitized image. However, the provision of any copy, without the permission of the owner of the copyright of the manuscript, constitutes a breach of copyright which is an offence in law. In the case of Church of Ireland records there are a number of copyright owners. The older parish registers (registers of baptisms and marriages up to the end of 1870 and marriages before 1845) are State copyright in the Republic of Ireland and crown copyright in Northern Ireland, and the permission of the National Archives and the Public Record Office in Belfast, respectively, is required before copies from these records may be obtained. Similarly the copyright of civil registers of marriage (those from 1845 on) is controlled by the Registrars General in Dublin and Belfast. The copyright of virtually all the remaining archives of parishes, dioceses, cathedrals and central church bodies is vested in the Representative Church Body and is administered through the Librarian and Archivist in the Representative Church Body Library in Dublin. In the case of the

1 J.H. Baxter & Charles Johnston, *Medieval Latin word-list from British and Irish sources* (London, 1934).
2 For example, E.E. Thoyts, *How to read old documents* (Christchurch, 1971) provides a commentary on various types of documents with illustrations of different types of writing and tables of letter shapes, as does L.C. Hector, *The handwriting of English documents* (Dorking, 1980).

papers of organizations and individuals which have been deposited in libraries and archives, the copyright, unless specifically assigned to a repository, usually remains with those who created the records or their heirs in law, and it is the responsibility of the custodian of the records to ensure that there are no avoidable breaches of copyright. Most problems in the copyright area arise not from a refusal to copy a document for research purposes, for adequate notes can usually be made, but with requests for illustrative material for publication. In most cases the Representative Church Body seeks to be accommodating in the cases in which it owns the copyright of documents, portraits and photographs, but frequently the copyright is someone else's property, and in such circumstances the responsibility devolves on those who are seeking a copy to provide written permission from the copyright owner. If permission is granted for a copy to be made for a researcher, there will, almost invariably, be a cost which must be passed on the student. This may simply be the cost of providing the copy, but, in the case of all but the large national institutions, it is frequently more substantial than the average student, used only to subsidized photocopying charges in colleges, may be prepared for. If material has already been photographed or microfilmed, the costs of providing prints or print-outs from negatives are not considerable, but if the documents have to photographed or microfilmed for the first time then the cost will usually be passed on to the person who requested the copies. Since such operations will usually involve contracting the work out to professionals, the costs may on occasions be considerable, and students would be wise to obtain an estimate before ordering any illustrative material. Some repositories will allow readers to take their own photographs under supervision, but this option cannot be relied on. Finally, researchers should realize that most copyright owners are now aware that archives and their copyright are assets and, in an age of growing pressure for repositories to generate income, there is an increasing tendency to require the payment of reproduction fees.

If, however, when all the hurdles of research and interpretation have been overcome, the project still needs an initial boost, then students might look for a model on which to base their work. Happily there are a number of published histories of parishes, dioceses and cathedrals which clearly demonstrate how to proceed. These all have the common virtues of being soundly based on church records, of demonstrating the added value of wide reading, and of being logically constructed. At parish level, John Crawford's history of the Dublin parish of St Catherine[3] is exactly what the sub-title claims – a portrait of a Church of Ireland community – while Brendan Twomey's study of another Dublin parish, St Paul's,[4] places more emphasis on a wider concept of the parish as both a religious and a civil administrative unit. In the world of diocesan history Miriam Moffitt's study of the Church of Ireland community in Killala and Achonry[5] demonstrates how the Church in rural

---

3 John Crawford, *St Catherine's parish, Dublin, 1840–1900: portrait of a Church of Ireland parish* (Dublin, 1996). **4** Brendan Twomey, *Smithfield and the parish of St Paul, Dublin, 1698–1750* (Dublin, 2005). **5** Miriam Moffitt, *The Church of Ireland community of Killala & Achonry, 1870–1940* (Dublin, 1999).

Ireland can be fruitfully examined, while John Crawford's more substantial study of the Church of Ireland in Victorian Dublin[6] is a model of how to handle large amounts of information, balance narrative and analysis, and produce a cogent and cohesive story. Most compelling of all is the multi-authored history of Christ Church cathedral, Dublin,[7] and, on a more modest level, the history of St Brigid's cathedral, Kildare,[8] both of which show how evidence can be used creatively to tell the story of an institution over a protracted period of time. What all these studies clearly show is that the history of the Church of Ireland is not just about buildings and administration but about how these structures were part of the lives of people who created them and who in turn had their lives moulded by them.

6 John Crawford, *The Church of Ireland in Victorian Dublin* (Dublin, 2005).   7 Kenneth Milne (ed.), *Christ Church cathedral, Dublin: a history* (Dublin, 2000).   8 Raymond Gillespie (ed.), *St Brigid's cathedral, Kildare: a history* (Maynooth, 2001).

Conclusion

The Church of Ireland, as the legal lineal descendant of the early Irish Church, has inherited responsibility for a collection of archives and manuscripts which are an important part of the national heritage. Despite losses of significant parts of the collection through accident, neglect and the periodic instability to which Irish society was subject, there remains in the custody of the Church and in the libraries of other institutions, to which items have migrated throughout the ages, a body of manuscript material, the understanding of which is essential for any effective analysis of the history of Irish society. Because the Church was organized locally through parishes, dioceses and cathedrals, its records are particularly valuable for those engaged in the study of local history; and because the Church of Ireland became the official Church of the State, it had a presence throughout the country which was more widespread and more influential than its position, as a minority Church, would otherwise have made possible.

The surviving body of records, substantial though it is, represents only a fraction of that which once existed. Nevertheless information which has been lost can, to some extent, be recovered through the use of copies and extracts and by exploring supplementary sources such as inscriptions on gravestones, memorials and plate, and the evidence of archaeology and architecture. In addition, the pioneering work of scholars, principally in the late nineteenth and early twentieth centuries, in producing printed editions and calendars of archives and manuscripts has saved for posterity texts which otherwise would have been lost, especially in the light of the archival holocaust at the Four Courts in Dublin in 1922.

Subsequent work by scholars, archivists, librarians and committed amateur historians has produced a substantial body of catalogues, guides, lists and descriptive articles which can be used to interpret, in part, a wide variety of Church of Ireland archives and manuscripts. However, much material has yet to be catalogued and, given the unpredictable nature of Irish archival life, perhaps some valuable material may remain to be discovered. In both these fields of endeavour local historians have a valuable role to play. They, through their interest and enthusiasm, can set an agenda for local research to which archivists and librarians can, within the constraints under which they work, respond. More importantly, perhaps, they can, through their experience and expertise, help to develop a greater awareness of the centrality of Church of Ireland records to much local research. Together, those who have custody of the archives and manuscripts of the Church of Ireland and those who use them can be a formidable force for the development of local studies in Ireland.

Select bibliography

Akenson, D.H., *The Church of Ireland: ecclesiastical reform and revolution, 1800–1885* (New Haven & London, 1971)

Begley, D.F. (ed.), *Irish genealogy: a record finder* (Dublin, 1981).

Berry, H.F., *Register of the wills and inventories of the diocese of Dublin* (Dublin, 1898).

Bliss, W.H. (ed.), *Calendar of entries in the papal registers relating to Great Britain and Ireland* (London, 1893).

Church disestablishment 1870–1970: a centenary exhibition (Dublin, 1970).

John Crawford, *The Church of Ireland in Victorian Dublin* (Dublin, 2005).

Cross, F.L., & E.A. Livingstone (eds), *The Oxford dictionary of the Christian Church* (4th ed., Oxford, 2005).

Crossman, Virginia, *Local government in nineteenth century Ireland* (Belfast, 1994).

Deane, J.L.B., *Church of Ireland handbook* (2nd ed., Dublin, 1982).

Day, Angelique, & Patrick McWilliams (eds), *Ordnance survey memoirs of Ireland* (40 vols, Belfast, 1990–98).

Ecclesiastical commissioners, Ireland: reports, 1814, 1835, 1836, 1838.

Edwards, Kathleen, *The English secular cathedrals in the Middle Ages* (2nd ed., Manchester, 1967).

Gillespie, Raymond (ed.), *The first chapter act book of Christ Church cathedral, Dublin, 1574–1700* (Dublin, 1997).

——, *The vestry records of the parishes of St Catherine and St James, Dublin, 1657–1692* (Dublin, 2004).

Gurrin, Brian, *Pre-census sources for Irish demography* (Dublin, 2002).

Helferty, Seamus, & Raymond Refaussé (eds), *Directory of Irish archives* (4th ed., Dublin, 2003).

Hawkes, William, 'The liturgy in Dublin' in *Reportorium novum*, ii, no. 1 (1957–8), pp 33–67.

Hayes, R.J. (ed.), *Manuscript sources for the history of Irish civilization* (12 vols, Boston, 1964) & *Supplement* (3 vols, Boston, 1979).

Irish Church Directory, 1862–.

Irish Ecclesiastical Gazette, 1856–.

Lemberg, S.E., *The reformation of cathedrals: cathedrals in English society, 1485–1603* (Princeton, 1988).

Leslie, J.B., *Armagh clergy and parishes* (Dundalk, 1911).

Lewis, Samuel, *A topographical dictionary of Ireland* (2 vols & atlas, London, 1837).

Lists of oil paintings … in the possession of the bishops, deans, chapters and Representative Body of the Church of Ireland (Dublin, 1916).

McEnery, M.J., & Raymond Refaussé (eds), *Christ Church deeds* (Dublin, 2000).

Mills, James (ed.), *The register of St John the Evangelist, Dublin, 1619–1699* (Dublin, 1906, rep. 2000).

Milne, Kenneth, *A short history of the Church of Ireland* (4th ed., Dublin, 2003).

—— (ed.), *Christ Church cathedral, Dublin: a history* (Dublin, 2000).

—— (ed.), *A Church of Ireland bibliography* (Dublin, 2005).

Mitchell, Brian, *A new genealogical atlas* (Baltimore, 1988).

Papers of British churchmen (London, 1987).

Phillips, W.A. (ed.), *History of the Church of Ireland from the earliest times to the present day* (3 vols, Oxford, 1933).

Potterton, Homan, *Irish church monuments, 1570–1880* (Belfast, 1985).

Pounds, N.J.G., *A history of the English parish* (Cambridge, 2000).

Refaussé, Raymond, 'The archives of the Church of Ireland: an introduction' in *Irish Archives Bulletin*, xi (1981), pp 3–11;

——, 'The archives of the Church of Ireland and the Representative Church Body Library' in *Archivium Hibernicum*, xlix (1995), pp 115–24;

——, 'Church of Ireland clerical succession lists and their compilers' in *Irish Genealogist*, x, no. 1 (1998), pp 32–41.

——, 'Records of the Church of Ireland' in J.G. Ryan (ed.), *Irish Church records* (2nd ed., Dublin, 2001).

Refaussé, Raymond, & Mary Clark, *A catalogue of the maps of the estates of the archbishops of Dublin, 1654–1850* (Dublin, 2000).

Reid, Noel (ed.), *A table of Church of Ireland parochial registers and copies* (Naas, 1994).

Sheehy, M.P., *Pontifica Hibernica* (2 vols, Dublin, 1962 & 1965).

Tallon, Maura, *Church of Ireland diocesan libraries* Dublin, 1959).

Twomey, Brendan, *Smithfield and the parish of St Paul, Dublin, 1698–1750* (Dublin, 2005)

White, James, & Michael Wynne, *Irish stained glass* (Dublin, 1963).

Wood, Herbert, *A guide to the records deposited in the Public Record Office of Ireland* (Dublin, 1919).

Index